Choice

T0366527

Broadening Perspectives on Social Policy
Series Editor: Bent Greve

The object of this series, in this age of re-thinking on social welfare, is to bring fresh points of view and to attract fresh audiences to the mainstream of social policy debate.

The choice of themes is designed to feature issues of major interest and concern, such as are already stretching the boundaries of social policy.

This is the thirteenth collection of papers in the series. Previous volumes include:

Choice

Challenges and Perspectives for the European Welfare States

Edited by

Bent Greve

A John Wiley & Sons, Ltd., Publication

This edition first published 2010
Originally published as Volume 43, No. 6 of *Social Policy Administration*
Chapters © 2010 The Authors
Book compilation © 2010 Blackwell Publishing Ltd

Blackwell Publishing was acquired by John Wiley & Sons in February 2007. Blackwell's publishing program has been merged with Wiley's global Scientific, Technical, and Medical business to form Wiley-Blackwell.

Registered Office
John Wiley & Sons Ltd, The Atrium, Southern Gate, Chichester, West Sussex, PO19 8SQ, United Kingdom

Editorial Offices
350 Main Street, Malden, MA 02148-5020, USA
9600 Garsington Road, Oxford, OX4 2DQ, UK
The Atrium, Southern Gate, Chichester, West Sussex, PO19 8SQ, UK

For details of our global editorial offices, for customer services, and for information about how to apply for permission to reuse the copyright material in this book please see our website at www.wiley.com/wiley-blackwell.

The right of Bent Greve to be identified as the author of the editorial material in this work has been asserted in accordance with the Copyright, Designs and Patents Act 1988.

All rights reserved. No part of this publication may be reproduced, stored in a retrieval system, or transmitted, in any form or by any means, electronic, mechanical, photocopying, recording or otherwise, except as permitted by the UK Copyright, Designs and Patents Act 1988, without the prior permission of the publisher.

Wiley also publishes its books in a variety of electronic formats. Some content that appears in print may not be available in electronic books.

Designations used by companies to distinguish their products are often claimed as trademarks. All brand names and product names used in this book are trade names, service marks, trademarks or registered trademarks of their respective owners. The publisher is not associated with any product or vendor mentioned in this book. This publication is designed to provide accurate and authoritative information in regard to the subject matter covered. It is sold on the understanding that the publisher is not engaged in rendering professional services. If professional advice or other expert assistance is required, the services of a competent professional should be sought.

Library of Congress Cataloging-in-Publication Data

Choice : challenges and perspectives for the European welfare states / edited by Bent Greve.
    p. cm. – (Broadening perspectives in social policy)
  Includes bibliographical references and index.
  ISBN 978-1-4443-3331-2 (pbk.)
  1. Social choice–Europe. 2. Welfare state–Europe. 3. Consumers' preferences–Europe. I. Greve, Bent.
  HB846.8.C47 2010
  361.6'5094–dc22

                        2010009776

A catalogue record for this book is available from the British Library.

Set in 10.5 on 11 pt Baskerville by Toppan Best-set Premedia Limited
Printed and bound in Malaysia by Vivar Printing Sdn Bhd

01   2010

CONTENTS

NOTES ON CONTRIBUTORS

Florian Blank is Researcher in the Graduate School of Politics, Westfälische Wilhelms-Universität Münster, Germany.

Melanie Eichler is based at the Centre for Globalization and Governance, University of Hamburg, Germany.

Menno Fenger is Assistant Professor at the Department of Public Administration, Erasmus University Rotterdam, The Netherlands.

Paolo R. Graziano is Assistant Professor in the Department of Institutional Analysis and Public Management at Bocconi University, Milan, Italy.

Ian Greener is Reader in the School of Applied Social Sciences, University of Durham, UK.

Bent Greve is Professor at the Department of Society and Globalization at the University of Roskilde, Denmark.

Birgit Pfau-Effinger is Professor at the Institute of Sociology, University of Hamburg, Germany.

Martin Powell is Professor of Health and Social Policy at the Health Services Management Centre, University of Birmingham, UK.

Kirstein Rummery is Professor in the Department of Applied Social Sciences, University of Stirling, Scotland.

Steven Saxonberg is Professor of Sociology in the Department of Social Policy and Social Work at the Masaryk University in Brno, Czech Republic.

Deborah Wilson is Senior Research Fellow, CMPO, University of Bristol, UK.

Editorial Introduction

Bent Greve

'Choice, choice and more choice' has been a buzzword in many welfare states around Europe in recent years. This has transformed the welfare states in the direction of a more market-oriented approach, changed users into consumers and increased the emphasis on private providers. Expectation of higher responsiveness from the provider has been part of the reasons for change. Delivery of welfare services has in many countries seen a split between who finances and who provides. Furthermore, the starting point for this development has been the constant focus on increased effectiveness of the public sector in all types of welfare states. The boundary between the public and private sectors is consequently less distinct than it used to be.

More choice has been linked to an increase in competition between welfare providers, including also areas with public delivery only, ensuring intra-organizational competition. Competition has been introduced in various ways, including the application of per-user funding, vouchers and tax credits. However, the establishment of free choice has rarely been associated with an analysis of the consequences of introducing choice.

These consequences relate to whether free choice in fact increases competitiveness, improves efficiency, changes user empowerment or has an impact on equality of access to central welfare services. Neglected in the analysis has thus often been the possibly negative impact of choice, including the potential increase in stress when people are obliged to choose. Questions about whether transaction costs have increased more than any possible efficiency gain have received more scant attention.

This book describes and analyses recent change with regard to free choice from a theoretical and empirical perspective. Theoretically, this is done by discussing conditions for choice and, especially, the Third Way understanding of the impact of choice. Empirically, it is done by concrete analysis of a variety of choices in the welfare states in Europe, and also of specific sectors (such as education, health, day care and long-term care) in the welfare states, including choice of provider and type of services. Gender implications and the impact of choice are also central to several chapters in this book.

The combination of theoretical and empirical articles, within different spheres of the welfare states, informs us about core changes in the welfare states including the actual use of choice, and why choice is used or not used. Empirical analysis is needed because equality, for example, cannot only be understood and measured with regard to economic parameters. Analysis is needed also to study equality of access and the possibility of using choice, including the possibility of having an informed free choice. The relationship to the New Public Management and change in the public sector has also been central for several of the chapters.

The book starts with a chapter by Bent Greve setting the scene for what type of conditions need to be fulfilled in order to ensure an informed choice for users, without negative impact on equality, especially in access to services. One of the conclusions of the chapter is that, although certain conditions that need to be fulfilled can be presented, empirical analysis – sector by sector, provision by provision – is necessary in order to ascertain the precise impact on equality, efficiency and cost related to free choice.

Julian Le Grand has been one of the proponents of the expansion of choice in Third Way politics in the UK. He was also among the first to analyse the conditions that must be fulfilled in a quasi-market in order to ensure a properly functioning choice system. In the chapter by Ian Greener and Martin Powell, Le Grand's earlier and later writings in relation to choice and quasi-markets are explored. This chapter thus at the same time provides a strong overview of one of UK's leading social policy analysts, and also reflects upon why changes in the original positions of Le Grand, especially from 1992 to 2007, have taken place. Le Grand's historical worry concerning equality of access and the functioning of welfare markets has presumably changed towards an understanding that competition in itself within the public sector 'serves the public interest better than trusting professionals'. Greener and Powell thus argue that focus seemingly has changed from the critique of market-based reform to one of public sector delivery.

One of the sectors where choice has been expanded in several countries is education. In the UK, voice is now seen as central for the user's ability to influence the educational sector, as Deborah Wilson argues in her chapter. The analysis is carried out by going back to Hirschman's original work on exit, voice and loyalty, which is then applied to the English educational sector. In this way the chapter shows how to interpret and use classical understanding in a modern context. The chapter argues that, although voice and choice should be able to complement each other, this has not been the case in the UK, or at least only for a limited number of users. The meaning of quality in the service can also be understood differently, and thus the risk is that those more able to express their views might be more readily listened to by producers. This will implicitly and avoidably imply a new kind of inequality in the welfare states.

What choice is and when choice is not really a choice is, with a focus on Germany, the central core of the chapter by Florian Blank. The chapter offers a precise and clear overview of recent reform, especially from an institutional perspective. The chapter also argues that, although choice has not been at the forefront of the debate, it has gradually been introduced. Differences in the ways choice works are related to how closely it resembles the market's way of working, whether it is voluntary or obligatory, and the range of choices open to users. Quality of choice is also influenced by these institutional frames, which also include the way resources are calculated and distributed within the different spheres of social policies.

We move from Germany to Italy, where Paolo Graziano raises the question of whether recent reforms in the Italian welfare state have increased real choice for citizens. Thus, for example, the change in the pension system implies that the gross replacement rate will decline significantly, especially for those not using the option of saving in a supplementary occupational pension system. The option for choice might thus be an option for a lower pension and, thereby, imply new inequalities in the welfare states. Opportunity and choice might therefore be possible only for a more limited group in society.

The impact of choice is also the focus of the next chapter, by Melanie Eichler and Birgit Pfau-Effinger, who ask the question why, despite more choice in care for elderly people in Germany, it is still the case that the majority of those needing care are looked after by family members. Cultural values embedded in who has the responsibilities in the families, it is argued, are the main basis for this. Family care is perceived by the users as the best-quality care, making choice or use of choice a less relevant issue. This is documented by qualitative analysis using 33 interviews with women carrying out care for families in the years 2004 and 2005. The chapter thus highlights that choice in itself is not sufficient to change attitudes and behaviour, and that this also should be taken into consideration when implementing choice. Furthermore, trust and good personal relations can be highly important, especially with regard to care.

A comparative analysis of the impact of choice, especially for people with disabilities, when moving towards cash-for-care is analysed by Kirstein Rummery. The chapter includes a comparison between the UK, the Netherlands, France, Italy, Austria and the USA. A clear conclusion is that market solutions can offer positive effects for both users and carers if the state continues to have a strong impact and influence on the programmes, at the same time providing users and providers with the possibility of exercising choice and control. If, on the other hand, this does not happen, there will be a negative impact on gender equality, and certain users might have difficulties. Cash-for-care seems to be especially suited to the young and better-educated. This points to the dilemma between the possible negative impact on social division and the empowerment of some users.

The risk for individuals when choice systems offer exit options from previously mandatory programmes is analysed in the chapter by Menno Fenger. The possible consequences in relation to adverse selection are examined in relation to welfare policies in four European countries: the Netherlands, Spain, Sweden and the UK. The impact of opting out is different in each of these areas. Pensions are a case where opt-out has been prominent, but despite this no clear pattern of adverse selection has been observed. Still, opting out has only been introduced in a more limited way in recent years in the four countries, and might in the years to come be a consequence of more choice in welfare states around Europe.

Choice and the freedom to choose lifestyle are analysed through a study by Steven Saxonberg of how the promotion of gender equality might have an impact on choice in families. Differences in family policy, including access to day care and parental leave, have an impact on the choices families can make. The more gender-neutral Nordic welfare states have been better able to pursue real freedom of choice in daily life. Welfare services can thus influence the possibility of having a real free choice within the family and between men and women in the welfare states.

The chapter taken together point towards remarkable change in welfare states in Europe – changes that imply new dividing lines caused by the use of markets and marketization as a consequence of more choice, but also implying that those not able to make choices in an informed way run the risk of less-good service. Inequalities in income or occupation could thus be expanded to be inequalities in the ability to manage choice. The risk is that social cohesion will be reduced given that, for some, choice is an option and has a positive impact. For others, more choice is less and might imply social exclusion.

Choice can therefore have positive empowerment elements for the users. However, the risk observed in several European countries has been profound, for example, in that it implies new dividing lines of inequality and that choice is not possible for all. In particular, the ability to make an informed choice based upon clear and systematic information is far from the case for everybody. An eye on the possible negative impact of increasing choice, due to market failure, is thus still essential.

1
Can Choice in Welfare States Be Equitable?

Bent Greve

Introduction

Choice and increased choice have been at the core of the debates and changes in welfare states in Europe. This development has been observed across traditional understandings of welfare regimes. Increase in choice has not only been seen in liberal models with an already high emphasis on markets and marketization of welfare issues, but the choice revolution has arrived also in universal welfare states such as Sweden and Denmark (Blomqvist 2004). Choice is shifting the consumer from a passive recipient to an active choice-maker (Mann 2005). Choice is thus at the outset a good thing, as Appleby *et al.* have expressed it: 'who could argue against the desirability of allowing patients more say in decisions concerning them' (2003: 2). Choice has increasingly been on the agenda, partly because electorates are increasingly willing to choose private alternatives, including in the health and pensions areas (Ross 2000). However, the question is: Will more choice in all welfare sectors and in any conditions be positive for societal development? Furthermore, it might be the case that more choice in fact is less choice (Schwartz 2004).

'Positive for societal development' will be understood as related to a higher or at least a stable degree of equity in access to welfare services. The analysis of this depends on how one looks at equity and what the outcomes are. It might be considered that expanding choice is about enhancing equity and opportunity (Le Grand 2007). It has also been argued that 'choice and control that is facilitated as an outcome of social care … has the most significant impact on experiences of independence, well-being and social inclusion' (Glendinning 2008: 461). The counter-argument is that it is of no use to have a choice if, for reasons that will be described later, it is not possible to use it, or the real option of choice is there only for some users, and also that choice understood in this way can be highly individualistic.

Choice could also be 'positive for societal development' if it implied a more efficient delivery. This will, although a more limited consideration, also be discussed (cf., for example, the section on transaction costs, below).

The focus in this chapter is on conditions that must be fulfilled in order to ensure a free and well-informed choice, but also on the impact on equity under different conditions for choice. Equity is understood as equality in the ability to exercise choice and gain access to welfare state services. Access is further understood not only as a formal right to access; there is also a requirement that informal barriers (such as the possible cost of using the right to choose – for example, transport costs and other transaction costs) are not a hindrance for an individual exercising choice. For some it is not the cost, but the difficulty in travelling which can be a hindrance (Exworth and Peckham 2006). Equity can also be achieved when increased choice reduces waiting lists and thus presumably makes access to service more equitable. This has, for example, been shown to be the case in one analysis from the UK (Dawson *et al.* 2004). Equity, it has been argued, is a reason for choice (Le Grand 2006), but it is also differently distributed dependent on class and income (Giddens 1998b).

Choice has been argued to be possible in principle in all sectors and all welfare areas. Markets or market mechanisms have been seen as the core ability to ensure a proper balance between demand and supply, and the best method to ensure correct revelation of the citizen's preferences. Disorganization of care has been observed in this process (Bode 2007). With regard to welfare state goods, the centre of attention has especially been on the right to choose between different types of service and service-providers. However, choice in relation to income transfers such as pensions has also been an area of growing interest in relation to both the type of pension scheme and its components. Choice seemingly has its root in neo-liberal reform strategies (Fotaki 2007), but has also been in line with strategies on empowerment. Choice has further been introduced without any evidence that this would make the welfare state more effective (Thomson and Mossialos 2006).

Choice in the welfare state can therefore be understood from various and very diverse perspectives. It ranges from neo-liberal, to empowerment of the vulnerable, to third way politics. Thus, for example, 'the third way politics in the UK was an extension of the market, but also creation of quasi-markets in the public sector and a choice of suppliers in education, health and social care' (Jordan 2005). This was put extremely clearly by Tony Blair in 2004: 'Choice puts the levers in the hands of the parents and patients so that they as citizens and consumers can be a driving force for improvement in their public services' (Tony Blair, *Guardian*, 24 June 2004). Further, it has been argued that people are consumers only in the market domain; in the public domain they are citizens (Le Grand 2007). The choice agenda thus had the ambition to 'reconcile the social democratic conception of a free, universal health service with a range of modernising strategies that draw on private sector investment and resources' (Newman and Vidler 2006: 103). The logic is, in general, that citizens would like to have the same kind of choice in the NHS and other welfare areas as in the market, but perhaps without a clear understanding that the private sector might also have problems with delivery.

Choice in delivery of services can also be understood as part of reflexive modernity (Beck 1992). Giddens has pointed out that there is a need to find a new balance between individual and collective responsibilities (Giddens

1998a). As part of the move towards choice, there is a drive to empower consumers and ensure they have a louder voice (Clarke 2005).

Public choice theory has, as another approach, pointed out that increase in individual choice is important so that delivery can be made in the way the user wants it, and not how the bureaucracy would like it (Mueller 2003). In addition, the New Public Management tradition has pointed to choice as part of the process of increasing efficiency by the pressure it can place on providers. Part of this reflects Tiebout's original description of voting with the feet as a possible part of the choice revolution, and an alternative to democracy (Cullis and Jones 1998).

However, choice is not something which just takes place freely and out of context, as the following indicates:

> By getting children to harvest, prepare and cook healthy meals, he managed to get them to eat food they would not previously even taste … [the argument further being that children's choice was used] as the excuse for providing unhealthy junk meals. Children's preferences were culturally determined; by changing the context, he changed the choices. (Jordan 2005: 438)

This is an example of a wider societal impact and shows that the conditions and context for choice have an impact on what type of choice is made, and how. Therefore, choice is not only something left for the market to have a say in, but can also be influenced by other actors, e.g. both civil society and the state. This is not only about choice, in itself and between providers, but also about the way systems are developing, and about ensuring the possibility for different individuals to make an informed choice. When moving from a perspective that is not focused only on the way the market works, but also on the impact on equity and on society, new perspectives for the impact of choice open up. This is further relevant, as the whole issue of choice has been developed by the impact on welfare delivery, and as a consequence of that 'business jargon capturing both welfare bureaucracies and non-statutory agencies involved in service provision' (Bode 2006: 346).

Furthermore, the way choice is made can be based upon types of heuristic. Availability heuristic is the influence of choice based on latest occasions, for example, how easy it was to get in contact, or get an appointment, the length of waiting time, etc. Representative heuristic focuses on our making choices based upon our preconceptions or stereotypes of a given situation, for example, how we expect primary education to be (Fotaki et al. 2005).

Social changes and individualism are seemingly moving societies towards a consumer culture with regard also to welfare state issues, but in this context the choice can be both informed and manipulated. Regulation of supply has been part of policies in relation to, for example, drugs, alcohol and gambling. To put it another way, the free choice does not take place in a free and open market because society has decided to restrict choice in these areas. This further reflects the fact that restrictions on choice can be necessary as part of the optimization of societal welfare, here especially understood as equality in access to welfare service.

Finally, increased choice can for some people be a reason for a lower perceived living standard, as they might feel frustrated and stressed by having to make choices, and also by having the risk of making the wrong choice, which can have an impact on their daily life. For the individual a wrong choice regarding a new pair of trousers is irritating, but a wrong choice in saving for a pension can reduce one's economic security in old age (Schwartz 2004). The dire consequences for living standards in the future of making the wrong choice now can thus be a specific new type of risk in welfare states. This might happen despite full information in principle having been given, as not all people have the ability to use such information well in decision-making. Non-decision therefore often also becomes an option that many people take, as they believe that the implicit choice that others have made for them is the best one. The way choice is presented might thus have a huge impact on the final outcome.

Choice and choice in welfare states have many different aspects, and the variety can be understood as being in relation to:

- content of service (specification of inputs or outputs);
- level (quantity, perhaps subject to a charge above a certain threshold);
- identity of a gatekeeper (case manager, commissioners);
- provider. (6, 2003)

The rest of this chapter will focus on what conditions should be fulfilled in order to ensure a free and informed choice. At the same time it will focus on the impact on equity, including when equity and choice are on a divergent, and where on a convergent, path.

In general, six conditions should be fulfilled in order to ensure free choice without negative impact on equity (Greve 2003):

1. competitive market forces
2. sufficient and precise information
3. low transaction costs
4. precise incentive structure
5. avoidance of incentives to cream-skimming
6. trust in providers

The analysis in the following sections will revolve around these six conditions. In line with Hirschman (1970) one could also have focused on exit, voice and loyalty as possible options in a choice-based system. The question would then be: when and for whom especially is exit an option? Whether one can or cannot use Hirschman's three options is also part of the equity question. The possibility of using choice also to exit is therefore part of the conditions to be fulfilled if choice is not to imply a negative impact on user access to different types of welfare services.

Can a Competitive Market Be Ensured in Welfare Delivery?

Traditional economic analysis points to the importance of the need to have many buyers and many suppliers in order to ensure a competitive market.

Full information is also important; this will be returned to later. The question is thus: Is it possible to have many buyers and sellers in a welfare market?

Presumably, the answer will depend on the more specific aspect of the individual welfare product to be delivered, but also on many of the service aspects of the welfare market, including the difficulty of measuring and ensuring quality of the service over a long time. A more detailed knowledge of each individual area needs to be analysed, and it is not possible theoretically to find a final answer for all types of welfare services. Sometimes, it might take time to develop a market. This has, for instance, been the case in Denmark, where the number of people using a private provider of practical home help for elderly persons has risen from 17,054 (out of 166,371 eligible people) in 2004 to 39,507 (out of 141,568) in 2007. The private welfare sector has thus been rapidly expanding in this area. However, it has to be borne in mind that this is a sector with low demand for intensive capital investment to start up a company.

Specifically, the more care-oriented aspects of welfare delivery can be difficult to disentangle from the classical industrial product, where quality might be more easily measured. Care can, further, be very individual, and a common measure for both quality and quantity might not be so simple to find. Therefore, choice with regard to care, and the public sector's ability to ensure good-quality care, even when delivered by private providers, will be a new challenge. The vulnerable elderly in need of personal care will, for example, be in need of treatment even on the days when a private provider does not function. Furthermore, the public sector will have to ensure that monopolies are not also developed by private providers, given the risk of higher prices and/or lower quality if this happens.

The regulatory function in the public sector will thus need to be increased if marketization and the use of quasi-markets is increased, as has been the case when expanding choice in the welfare states. The regulator will further need to be aware not only of the cost aspect of the delivery, but also of the quality aspect and ensure that weaker groups also have access to high-quality services. The level of increased cost in relation to this depends on the degree of internal control in the public administration already established.

A competitive market, as argued in classical economic textbooks, is the most efficient way to deliver service, as this reflects the choice of individuals, and the choice in itself points to what the users want. However, even if the market is more effective in delivery of certain goods and services, the extra administrative burden can reduce societal gains by moving delivery from state to market (cf. the section on transaction costs, below).

A specific problem relates to the transformation from users to consumers. Consumerism changes the role of the individual, but the mixed economy might also have 'lost these qualities of fairness and responsibility' (Baldock 2003: 68). When one is a consumer and not a user, the right to complain and demand individual solutions increases. Part of the choice revolution, on the other hand, exactly reflects the wish to move away from a monopoly public provider to a more responsive provision of goods and services.

An ethical issue also arises as to the way to ensure the protection of those vulnerable people who might be 'misused' by being provided with a lower

9

quality of service than is reasonable, or than perhaps has been paid for by the individual or the public. It is thus important to establish methods of reducing cream-skimming, and this can be difficult (cf. below).

Even if there are problems related to creating a market, an argument in favour of choice has been that 'it reduces the role of the middle-class voice in allocating health resources' (Le Grand 2006: 704). It is, however, difficult to measure this, as the ability of the middle class to press for higher levels of spending is often balanced by tight management of welfare spending, and in recent years developments in spending, including in the area of health care, do not support the thesis.[1]

Still, the balance between empowerment and the ability to act and use freedom as consumers, given extended choice, is important. Will the weaker groups, by being in a better economic position, also be in a stronger position *vis-à-vis* providers, or do other aspects also have an impact on the possibility of exercising choice, such as educational attainment level. This again needs to be empirically analysed from case to case, from country to country, and also from the varieties of different types of context.

Finally, if a competitive market can be ensured in relation to choice, this implies that a producer who has not been chosen must expect to leave the market. This implies that the choices of other users can have a negative impact on those who preferred this producer, as they will have to find another producer, and this might well turn out to be one they already know that they do not prefer or have less trust in. The possibility that a provider might be forced out of the market also implies a need for the public sector, at least in certain welfare areas, such as care for the elderly, to have a 'back-up'. It also implies a need for a regulatory function to ensure that the contract is fulfilled, and its quality.

Sufficient and Precise Information

A competitive market can only function if there is full and precise information easily accessible for all users. Information can be costly for providers to make available and this will increase the price of the products. Not all users will be able to understand information in every field where they have the option to make a choice. All providers might not be prepared, for a variety of reasons, to provide the information or at least the necessary and correct information, and if they do provide it some will charge for it. Information, and the ability to understand and make decisions based upon information, can thus be a reason for increased inequity in a choice welfare system.

Asymmetrical information can further increase the risk of that those less informed will lose out. This is not the case only in very complicated areas such as pensions, but can also be the case for more 'ordinary' types of care. One would need information on the relative quality of providers, and one should also be aware that 'exercising choice does not necessarily need a lot of knowledge, but informed choice does' (Appleby *et al.* 2003: 24).

Even if information is available, it might be the case that the amount of information makes it difficult for some to make the choice. This can, as an example from the financial sector, be due to the fact that 'participants with limited financial experience are demotivated to make an individual selection when being confronted with a bewildering range of over 600 alternatives' (Hinrichs 2004: 44).

Providing information in areas where consumers do not have the necessary background to make an informed choice might thus be very difficult. This can be shown by the fact that when people are offered choice, but at the same time are told that if they do not choose they will be given a specific option, then most people in fact do not make a choice, but instead implicitly choose the package decided by the supplier. Overstating or understating the impact of choice can also have an effect. This is, for example, the case in the health-care sector, as 'risk information can also be subject to manipulation to produce different decisions or interpretations by the patient' (Fotaki *et al.* 2005: 16).

Deciding not to make a choice will thus also have an impact, and, if the information is presented in such a way that it points towards specific types of choice, this will be the outcome. Non-decision might thus be the most common choice, and so no real choice has been enabled. It could be important to take into consideration the complexities of the area in question before embarking upon the development of increased choice in welfare states. The very complex decisions, for example about the use of different types of medicine, should therefore be taken by a specialist.

Low Transaction Costs

The cost involved in increasing choice in welfare delivery is an important aspect of the choice agenda. Change in cost can be a consequence of increased choice for both providers and users, and thus also for society as a whole.

The increase in cost relates to, at the least, the following elements: information, control, excessive supply, increased transport, time to implement choice, a new type of administration. The new type of cost arises because, when welfare services were delivered by the public sector, a clearer link existed between provider and users, whereas in a choice model, and especially when private providers are included, an extra link has to be included. This is needed in order to ensure that persons have the right to the service, but also that quality and price for the service are well known to all. Furthermore, the provider needs to know what it will receive in income, the criteria for receiving payment and the incentives it will have in the way the choice is organized.

If there are user charges, this will imply three different but interlinked set of prices for producer, public sector and user which all in their way can have an impact on who can make choices and the total level of societal cost of the provision of the service. The making of contracts will therefore also be more important than it presumably has been in the classical provision of welfare. Finally, there might be administrative costs related to handling user charges.

This is not the place to go into details about cost and its calculation. The intention has been to point out that it is an issue which can have an impact on equity. It can, however, be argued that, even though increased cost can be the consequence of choice, this has to be compared to increased efficiency and the consumer surplus created by having choice.

The list of extra costs above does not include the possible psychological stress factors arising from choice (Schwartz 2004), but, theoretically, one should include these, as for some they can be a problem. Making a choice implies the risk of making a wrong choice, which can, for example, have a devastating impact in the area of pensions. On the other hand, if choice increases well-being then this can be a reason for expanding choice (Jordan 2006).

Still, from an equity point of view it is important that the cost of making the choice is not prohibitive for the individual. For example, 'if no or little help with transport costs is offered, then inequalities in utilization are likely to be exacerbated by patient choice' (Le Grand 2006: 703). From a societal point of view, the total transaction cost of more choice should also be measured against the benefits achieved by a given choice, as the transaction cost could have been used instead to deliver welfare.

Precise Motivational Structure

As welfare services are not the same as many private goods, and as it is important for societies to have several of these services (for example, health care), then even if it is not compatible with market delivery, there is a need to ensure that a clear motivational structure for suppliers is in place. Different types of incentive structure are at play ranging from a fee per user, types of capitation fees, bottom or top income limits, etc. What works in one area might in fact not work in other areas, given the differences in number of users, sunk costs related to the area, quality requirements, etc. There is also a need to ensure that the producers have incentives to treat all clients.

Furthermore, this is an area where the classical problem with regard to principal/agent is in place (Rees 1985). That is to say, in relation to choice, the agent does not reveal all knowledge to the principal, in order to be in the best possible position. The relation between principal and agent is in many ways the same in principle whether we are talking about a public or private provider, but the possibilities for internal control are higher when delivery is inside a public organization compared to how it is with regard to private providers. This increases the need for specified contracts and agreements if using private providers (cf. the section on transaction costs, above).

This is not to say that motivation cannot be achieved, but it increases the complexity in the relation between decision-makers and providers of different kinds of services. Another issue with regard to the principal–agent relationship is the risk of cream-skimming (cf. the next section).

Incentives to Cream-skimming Are Avoided

A provider will have the incentive to cream-skim as this puts the provider in the best situation.[2] In a free-choice system the risk is that the provider will, if it can or is allowed to, pick the best lemon (Akerlof 1970). This might make it more difficult for persons who are in need of complicated treatment or care to access this. If the more 'difficult' cases are not skimmed away by providers, another risk is that providers use cream-skimping, i.e. reducing the quality of the treatment for the individual patient (Propper *et al.* 2006). Therefore, an important prerequisite for the functioning of a proper system is that the right incentives for providers are in place (cf. also the section on motivational structures, above). This can be the right price, conditions for receiving users etc.

In the health-care sector, methods to avoid cream-skimming can, for example, be:

1. stop-loss insurance, e.g. if a patient is very expensive, more resources will be given;
2. users have no choice, and the provider will have to take all patients referred to them;
3. risk-adjust the pricing system (but this is a complex and difficult measure);
4. tariff for treatment inversely with a deprivation index. (Le Grand 2006)

None of these is simple to implement, and they can have a negative impact on other aspects. For example, even a simple suggestion that the provider will have to take all patients referred to them might imply longer waiting lists, or that the treatment will be less thorough than otherwise.

It seems possible, though not simple, to find systems in the different areas of the welfare state to help in ensuring that cream-skimming is, if not avoided, then reduced (Barros 2003). Still, choice raises new issues in relation to the steering of the welfare state if the idea is to ensure access for all.

Trust

This section will, albeit briefly, look into trust as an element in guaranteeing that the outcome of choice from both society and individual users' point of view can be considered as useful. The analysis will not deal with how trust can be understood as a concept (cf. Sztompka 1999), and the possible relation between social capital and trust will not be included.

Trust in delivery will be an important condition for having a functioning choice system if the cost of the system is to be reduced, as trust would reduce the need for detailed control systems. Trust has been seen as an element that could reduce uncertainty and thereby increase efficiency (Bartlett *et al.* 1998). A core issue is that 'if individual choices and spontaneously created bonds cannot be relied upon to create stable institutions, let alone sustainable and just ones, what kinds of social units, of what size, based on which values, should be nurtured, and by which policies?' (Jordan 2005: 428).

Trust is therefore an important aspect in ensuring that, on the one hand, choice can be effective and, on the other hand, that misuse of the individual does not take place, for example, that more vulnerable people or those less familiar with making choices get what they have a right to and that it is of sufficiently high quality.

Trust is not only trust in delivery; if users have a 'lack of understandable and trusted information, [they] do not engage with the choice they have, and as a consequence, make no choice at all' (Mann 2005: 82).

Trust can be established, trust can be destroyed and trust can be misused. This implies that ensuring trust is not something one can just do and then expect that the trust will remain in the future. Misuse of trust happens when a supplier, for example in relation to care, first establishes a trustworthy position, and then reduces the quality when it has become difficult for the consumer to change supplier. Given that many choices in fact are based upon non-decisions, then trust in those providing the information on which the choice is made is extremely important. Therefore, information should not be left to the providers of the services, but should be based upon a common concept and be under public control.

Equity

The issue of equity has been running through the sections above, so this section is intended mainly to sum up and be more specific in relation to the interaction between choice and equity.

It has been argued that if policy-makers are concerned about equitable distributional outcomes – avoiding adverse selection and segregation – 'then they must be prepared to spend large sums, for none of the design solutions are cheap' (6, 2003: 265). This implies that if it can be indicated from the outset of an analysis that the expected outcome of a choice programme might have negative impact on equity in a society, then it is in fact the concrete specification and implementation of the programme that are important when trying to judge the impact on equity.

Nevertheless, the ability to make informed choices can be a very different thing, depending on, among other things, the social capital of the individual, but also on elements such as transport costs. Therefore, especially in the area of education and health care, inequalities seemingly arise (Greve 2002).

In the area of health care the inequalities can arise for several reasons: lack of ability to communicate, lack of ability to pay, but also differences in access to specialists in a continuously specializing health-care system – as Appleby *et al.* have expressed it: 'Choice is not a free good' (2003: 35). A specific problem to address is that if the choice results in a less positive outcome, how then should this situation be redressed (Glendinning 2008). In some areas choices are one-off, in others they can more easily be changed (meals on wheels, home-help, community care, etc.) (Bailey 2006).

Inequalities arising from choice can vary also among countries, given their geographical situation and the way a market-like system has developed. Therefore, it might be, as in Germany and France, that 'abolishing choice and making health insurance compulsory for the whole population is the most effective means of dealing with adverse selection – a conclusion which governments in both countries have recently reached' (Thomson and Mossialos 2006: 324).

This also implies that if 'public expenditure for the provision of social services significantly narrows income inequality' (Marical *et al.* 2006: 4), and this is especially due to the relatively uniform distribution of these services, then a movement towards a choice system (especially if payment for treatment is included) and increasing the difficulty of accessing the system will increase inequality. In general, 'it is the conditions under which choice schemes operate rather than choice itself which determine its positive and negative effects' (Bailey 2006: 13).

Conclusions

Choice has implications for the welfare states, and new types of inequities might be arising. Choice can also have an impact on the cost of delivery, as choice can only be possible if there is more than one thing to choose from. There is thus a risk of increase in, for example, health-care costs (Exworth and Peckham 2006), but also more generally in relation to the administration of the welfare state.

Choice can be a powerful tool for those able to make well-informed choices, and especially when this is possible without having extra transaction costs as a consequence. An argument for choice has been that the present welfare system already gives the middle class the best access, and that only choice can redress this imbalance (Le Grand 2006). In this way, the mere introduction of choice improves equity. However, whether this is the case in all areas of welfare provision can be questioned. At the same time it is important to stress that choice is not necessarily related to the classical conflict between public and private delivery. It is the mode of choice and the impact of choice that are important. Distributional outcome will to a large degree be dependent on who finances the welfare, and who decides who has access, but also on the individual's ability to make informed choices.

Even if choice is increasing the well-being and happiness of citizens, albeit in only some areas and in some aspects, having to make a choice can reduce satisfaction. However, at the same time, 'even people who feel dissatisfied because of the burden of choice might still feel that choice was important' (6, 2003: 243).

The impact on equity can be difficult to calculate based upon a clear theoretical approach, as this depends on the specific circumstances before the implementation of choice or more choice, the conditions in which it is imposed, the outcome after the introduction of choice and who is to pay the extra transaction costs (if they are not balanced by more efficiency) introduced by the changes. Choice thus needs to be analysed and discussed, based upon not only theoretical knowledge, but also concrete empirical cases, as it is this evidence which can facilitate making the best judgement of the outcome.

We do know, however, that choice without restrictions and rules will have a negative impact on equity, as the market, left to itself, will not ensure equality. The question is thus what degree of inequity policy-makers are willing to accept for more empowerment of users, more choice and perhaps (but not proven in all areas) a more effective delivery of welfare.

Choice will work in a market without market failure. However, this starting point is not useful when trying to depict areas for choice in welfare state delivery, as a large part of what the welfare state is delivering is due to market failure. Thus, using the market metaphor might lead to circular arguments, as the reasons for public intervention have to do with the lack (for a variety of different reasons) of a well-functioning market. Still, this cannot be used as an argument for not trying to increase choice, if choice can improve efficiency, happiness and user involvement. So, trying to get the situation on both the demand and supply sides to be as close as possible to the market is important, while at the same time being conscious of the need to ensure equity in access. Public financing and public decision on the rules regarding access and rights are therefore central to ensure that choice does not increase inequalities. The same applies to paying for transport costs, so that choice works, especially in less densely populated areas.

Notes

1. Cf. data from Eurostat and/or the OECD on developments in spending on welfare. Even including occupational welfare (Greve 2007), the tendency is not towards increased spending, as welfare has to be financed somehow.
2. Again, this is in principle the same whether the provider is public or private. The gains from cream-skimming can in one sector be profit, in another better working conditions, higher salaries, etc.

References

Akerlof, G. A. (1970), The market for lemons: qualitative uncertainty and the market mechanism, *Quarterly Journal of Economics*, 84: 488–500.

Appleby, J., Harrison, A. and Devlin, N. (2003), *What is the Real Cost of More Patient Choice?* London: King's Fund.

Bailey, S. J. (2006), Facilitating choice in English local government, *Economic Affairs*, 26, 1: 11–17.

Baldock, J. (2003), On being a welfare consumer in a consumer society, *Social Policy and Society*, 2, 1: 65–71.

Barros, P. P. (2003), Cream-skimming, incentives for efficiency and payment system, *Journal of Health Economics*, 22: 419–43.

Bartlett, W., Roberts, J. and Le Grand, J. (eds) (1998), *A Revolution in Social Policy? Quasi-markets in the Welfare State: The Emerging Findings*, Bristol: Policy Press.

Beck, U. (1992), *Risk Society: Towards a New Modernity*, London: Sage.

Blomqvist, P. (2004), Privatization of Swedish welfare services, *Social Policy & Administration*, 38, 2: 139–55.

Bode, I. (2006), Disorganized welfare mixes: voluntary agencies and new governance regimes in Western Europe, *Journal of European Social Policy*, 16, 4: 346–59.

Bode, I. (2007), New moral economies of welfare: the case of domiciliary elder care in Germany, France and Britain, *European Societies*, 9, 2: 201–27.

Clarke, J. (2005), New Labour's citizens: activated, empowered, responsibilized, abandoned? *Critical Social Policy*, 25, 4: 447–63.

Cullis, J. and Jones, P. (1998), *Public Finances and Public Choice*, 2nd edn, Oxford: Oxford University Press.

Dawson, D., Jacobs, R., Martin, S. and Smith, P. (2004), Is patient choice an effective mechanism to reduce waiting times? *Applied Health Economics and Health Policy*, 3, 4: 195–203.

Exworth, M. and Peckham, S. (2006), Access, choice and travel: implications for health policy, *Social Policy & Administration*, 40, 3: 267–87.

Fotaki, M. (2007), Patient choice in healthcare in England and Sweden: from quasi-market and back to market? A comparative analysis of failure in unlearning, *Public Administration*, 85, 4: 1059–75.

Fotaki, M., Boyd, A., Smith, L., *et al.* (2005), *Patient Choice and the Organisation and Delivery of Health Services: Scoping Review*, London: National Coordinating Centre for NHS Service Delivery and Organization, R&D (NCCSDO).

Giddens, A. (1998a), *The Third Way: The Renewal of Social Democracy*, Cambridge: Polity Press.

Giddens, A. (1998b), Risk society: the context of British politics. In J. Franklin (ed.), *The Politics of Risk Society*, Cambridge: Polity Press, pp. 23–35.

Glendinning, C. (2008), Increasing choice and control for older and disabled people: a critical review of new developments in England, *Social Policy & Administration*, 42, 5: 451–69.

Greve, B. (2002), *Vouchers. Nye styrings- og leveringsmåder i velfærdsstaten* [Vouchers. New management and delivery methods in the welfare state], Copenhagen: Djøf's Forlag.

Greve, B. (2003), When is choice possible in social security? *European Journal of Social Security*, 5, 4: 323–38.

Greve, B. (2007), *Occupational Welfare: Winners and Losers*, Cheltenham: Edward Elgar.

Hinrichs, K. (2004), *Active Citizens and Retirement Planning: Enlarging Freedom of Choice in the Course of Pension Reforms in Nordic Countries and Germany*, ZeZ-Arbeitspapier, 11, Bremen: Zentrum für Sozialpolitik.

Hirschman, A. O. (1970), *Exit, Voice, and Loyalty: Responses to Decline in Firms, Organizations, and States*, Cambridge, MA: Harvard University Press.

Jordan, B. (2005), New Labour: choice and values, *Critical Social Policy*, 25, 4: 427–46.

Jordan, B. (2006), *Social Policy for the Twenty-first Century: New Perspectives, Big Issues*, Cambridge: Polity Press.

Le Grand, J. (2006), Equality and choice in public services, *Social Research*, 73, 2: 695–710.

Le Grand, J. (2007), The politics of choice and competition in public services, *Political Quarterly*, 78, 2: 207–13.

Mann, K. (2005), Three steps to heaven? Tensions in the management of welfare: retirement pensions and active consumers, *Journal of Social Policy*, 35, 1: 77–96.

Marical, F., Mira d'Ercole, M., Vaalavuo, M. and Verbist, G. (2006), *Publicly Provided Services and the Distribution of Resources*, OECD Social and Labour Market Papers no. 45, Paris: OECD.

Mueller, D. C. (2003), *Public Choice III*, Cambridge: Cambridge University Press.

Newman, J. and Vidler, E. (2006), More than a matter of choice? Consumerism and the modernisation of health care. In L. Bauld, K. Clarke and T. Maltby (eds), *Social Policy Review 18: Analysis and Debate in Social Policy*, Bristol: Policy Press, pp. 101–20.

Propper, C., Wilson, D. and Burgess, S. (2006), Extending choice in English health care: the implications of the economic evidence, *Journal of Social Policy*, 35, 4: 537–57.

Rees, R. (1985), The theory of principal and agent: Part I, *Bulletin of Economic Research*, 37, 1: 3–26.

Ross, F. (2000), Interest and choice in the 'not quite so new' politics of welfare, *West European Politics*, 23, 2: 11–34.

Schwartz, B. (2004), *The Paradox of Choice: Why More Is Less*, New York: HarperCollins.

Bent Greve

G, P. (2003), Giving consumers of British public services more choice: what can be learned from recent history? *Journal of Social Policy*, 32, 2: 239–70.

Sztompka, P. (1999), *Trust: A Sociological Theory*, Cambridge: Cambridge University Press.

Thomson, S. and Mossialos, E. (2006), Choice of public or private health insurance: learning from the experience of Germany and the Netherlands, *Journal of European Social Policy*, 16: 315–27.

2
The Other Le Grand? Evaluating the 'Other Invisible Hand' in Welfare Services in England

Ian Greener and Martin Powell

Introduction

The debate over the future of welfare services in the UK is moving decisively towards the greater use of markets. Among the leading voices advocating such reforms has been that of Julian Le Grand. One of this country's most influential and important social policy writers, he has published a series of path-breaking and highly cited contributions since the 1970s (e.g. Le Grand and Robinson 1976; Le Grand 1982, 2003, 2007; Le Grand and Bartlett 1993). Le Grand has also crossed the divide between academia and politics to take part in important Commissions (Fabian Society 2000; IPPR 2001) and was a senior policy adviser to the Prime Minister, having to, in his words 'put my money where my mouth was' (Le Grand 2007: 2), and no longer hide behind a 'veneer of academic detachment'. Lipsey (2007: 174) terms Le Grand a 'passionate advocate for choice'.

Le Grand is part of a long and honourable tradition of academic government policy advisers such as Richard Titmuss and Brian Abel-Smith. He has every right to advocate choice solutions, just as others can advocate trust, targets and voice models (see Le Grand 2007: ch. 1). However, like David Lipsey (2005, 2007), whom Le Grand generously invited to contribute a critical commentary to his 2007 book), we present a 'sceptic's perspective'. This chapter presents a critical assessment of the development of Le Grand's books that analyses the use of markets in welfare areas, from the state versus market debate through quasi-markets to individual choice in personalized services, exploring the similarities and differences in his work over time. It uses books because they give a fuller-length exposition of his work, as well as an opportunity to see how it has developed over time. The chapter examines Le Grand's analytical template, his use of empirical evidence, and his policy conclusions. In particular, it critically examines his most recent work advocating individual choice in *The Other Invisible Hand* (Le Grand 2007) through the lens of his previous work – the earlier and 'other' Julian Le Grand.

Le Grand's Work

Julian Le Grand's contribution to social policy has been wide-ranging. His first major book, co-authored with Ray Robinson, had its origins in a course taught to first-year undergraduate social science students (Le Grand and Robinson 1976). This text has developed through a number of editions with Carol Propper joining the original authors (Le Grand *et al.* 1992) and a planned fourth edition that will include New Labour's reforms. In 1982 Le Grand published a major text on *The Strategy of Equality*, which questioned the degree of equality achieved by the welfare state (but see Powell 1995). Along with some highly cited articles (Le Grand 1991; Glennerster and Le Grand 1995), he then focused on quasi-markets in welfare (Le Grand and Bartlett 1993), contributing to texts that evaluated their use (e.g. Bartlett *et al.* 1998; Le Grand *et al.* 1998). His next theme was human behaviour, which examined producers in terms of knights and knaves, and users in terms of pawns and queens (Le Grand 2003; see also Le Grand 1997). Le Grand's latest contribution pursues these ideas, extending them into individual choice in personalized services (Le Grand 2007), and offers an intellectual argument that dovetails well with the present government's public sector reforms.

Four main elements of Le Grand's work are perhaps most worth accentuating. First, his work on the use of markets in welfare policy has been a long-standing interest, going as far back as the 1970s. Le Grand has written on the use of market mechanisms in welfare, therefore, for thirty years, and over that time has made a sizeable contribution to debates on their use. Second, Le Grand has explored how social policy as a discipline considers inequality, arguing that taken-for-granted assumptions that welfare institutions have made society more equal are not always borne out in practice. He has long questioned the assumption that bureaucratic allocation mechanisms are well suited to deliver equity for welfare state users. Third, his work on motivation and public policy has been widely cited and discussed, suggesting that it is necessary to explore how service users and professionals interact in service settings, and exploring the incentives available to each. Finally, Le Grand has published more theoretical, economics-derived understandings of the relationship between markets and equity, showing his long-standing concern with equity in market mechanisms, and perhaps best encapsulated in his contribution to what became known as market socialism.

This chapter will focus primarily on the first of Le Grand's contributions, his explorations of the use of markets in public policy. This area represents both his longest contribution and his most recent work, and so offers the opportunity to evaluate his thinking over a significant period of time. However, as his work is so interlinked, a consideration of his analysis of markets will clearly bring in other areas of his work as well. The central question the chapter attempts to answer is whether Le Grand's approach and conclusions have varied over time.

Le Grand's Analysis of Welfare Markets

One of the main analytical themes of Le Grand and Robinson (1976) was the issue of the market versus the state. After discussing society's aims of efficiency and equity, the next question to ask is what kind of system could meet those objectives. Since the private market system is the dominant means of providing the goods and services that we use in our everyday lives, it is the obvious place to begin an examination of alternative systems (1976: xvii). While there are efficiency arguments in favour of a 'pure market', there are a number of disadvantages of market allocation such as externalities, consumer ignorance, uncertainty, equity and the role of giving (1976: 35–43). The authors conclude that the importance of externalities, consumer ignorance, uncertainty and so on is ultimately an empirical question, and that the resolution of the issue of 'market versus non-market provision' will depend first upon empirical research, and then upon the values of the person or persons trying to decide the issue (1976: 50).

In Le Grand, Propper and Robinson (1992), the analysis typically proceeds under the headings of objectives, the market system, government policies and assessment. In each section an economics-derived framework outlines issues in relation to the objective of policy that usually involves efficiency and equity of some kind, then the market system is outlined, including problems of demand and supply, imperfect information, or even irrationality in social care; before present government policies are outlined, and an assessment made or conclusions drawn. In sum, the analysis lives up to the title of the book – this is an analysis of social problems using economic concepts.

A year later Le Grand and Bartlett edited a collection (1993) that examined the idea of quasi-markets using a similar framework that assessed their efficiency and equity, but also considered whether an increase in responsiveness occurred as a result of the use of market mechanisms, and who were given choice in the market, and what kind. The conclusion claims that, in order for quasi-markets to be a success, a number of factors need to be present: market structures need to be competitive, with many purchasers and many providers; both sides of the market need cheap and accurate information so that opportunism can be avoided; uncertainty needs to be avoided so that '[w]here the degree of uncertainty about the future state of the world is high, and where bounded rationality is a limiting factor on the formulation of complete contracts, the costs of contract information may outweigh the benefits which might be expected to arise from greater flexibility of market exchange between independent agents' (1993: 29); purchasers and providers have to be motivated by financial considerations; and cream-skimming must be restricted. In terms of what happens if one of these conditions is violated, 'then it does not necessarily imply that it is a second-best situation for the other to be met. They may compensate for one another – if there is a problem with information in a market, it may be better for providers and purchasers not to be motivated by financial gains' (1993: 34). This seems to be a call for the pragmatic use of markets.

In short, quasi-markets *can* give the best of both worlds, of the state and the market, in that they *can* yield the advantages of both systems while minimizing the disadvantages *if* certain conditions are satisfied. Le Grand and Bartlett (1993) claim that the conditions of market structure, information, transaction costs and uncertainty, motivation, and cream-skimming must be satisfied in order to produce successful outcomes in terms of efficiency, responsiveness, choice and equity. Le Grand did not write the empirical chapters on health in this collection, but has contributed to other verdicts (e.g. Roberts *et al.* 1998; Le Grand *et al.* 1998; Le Grand 2002; see also Powell 2003).

Le Grand's next major text focused on one of the conditions for market success – motivation (Le Grand 2003). He notes that in the classic welfare state, producers were regarded as knights and users were regarded as pawns, but in the 1980s and 1990s, they were regarded more as knaves and queens, respectively. He concludes that 'public policy should be designed so as to empower individuals: to turn pawns into queens' (2003: 163) – that they should become sovereign.

In his 2007 book, Le Grand utilizes a similar framework to the 1992 book, but this time as a tool to advocate the use of choice and markets in social policy, suggesting that competition serves the public interest better than trusting professionals, the use of targets, or using voice mechanisms.

We now focus on a comparison between the approach and conclusions of *The Economics of Social Problems* (Le Grand *et al.* 1992) and *The Other Invisible Hand* (Le Grand 2007). The justification for choosing these two books is that they both have discussion of a framework for analysing markets in public policy, as well as chapters where those frameworks are applied to specific areas of welfare such as health and education. The books have a great deal in common, taking the reader through a predefined framework to explore the use of markets in a range of public policy areas. Each book contains a chapter on health care, and so that will be explored in greater depth below, as well as being an area that remained particularly controversial in terms of its use of markets in public provision.

Comparing Le Grand's Analysis in 1992 and 2007

The Economics of Social Problems (1992)

The Economics of Social Problems has become a classic text, going through several editions and even changing its author team. First published in 1976, the 1992 edition will be examined here as it was the first that included analysis of an actual UK model for health care, thus incorporating both the theory and the practice of markets.

In the 1992 book, Le Grand (with co-authors Carol Propper and Ray Robinson) analyses health care under the headings of efficiency and equity, before turning to an exploration of the market system in health care. He then turns to an assessment of government policies in the field before providing a summary of his argument.

In terms of efficiency, Le Grand uses the marginal social benefit and marginal social cost model in a theoretical exploration of how many hospital beds should be provided, at what cost. He suggests that the 'fact that measuring the benefits from health care is difficult should not obscure the essential truth that it is impossible to make any reasonable decision concerning resource allocation in the health field without taking some view (however crude) of the benefits involved' (1992: 41). The alternative, Le Grand suggests, is to 'rely on what may often be ill-informed and arbitrary assessments' (1992: 41). Efficient health care is about maximizing 'the difference between benefits and costs' (1992: 41).

In his analysis of equity, he provides three different definitions; that of minimum standards of treatment for those in need; a full equality definition in terms of equal treatment for equal need; and equality of access, which he notes is often poorly defined, but seems to be 'in terms of the costs or sacrifices that people have had to make to get medical care' (1992: 42).

Moving on to his discussion of the market system and health care, Le Grand suggests that several arguments have been advanced suggesting that market allocation in this area is inefficient: uncertainty of demand, imperfect consumer information, and externalities. He works through each in turn.

Uncertainty of demand, Le Grand suggests, matters because of the high cost of health care, but can be mitigated through the use of insurance. However, there are two big problems with insurance models of health care: moral hazard and adverse selection. The 'existence of moral hazard and adverse selection will mean the insurance market will be more limited than if the insurance companies had full information about the actions of buyers. As a result, certain people will not be able to buy insurance and will not have cover against the costs of medical care' (1992: 44). A market for health care, then, is limited because of uncertainty of demand caused by inequities that result from uncertainty of demand.

Imperfect information is the second problem. Le Grand suggests that 'neither before nor after the treatment can consumers easily acquire information that will enable them to make an informed choice. Instead the supplier of medical care – the physician – is also the supplier of information. The supplier of care thus acts as the consumer's *agent*, informing her both about her illness and its treatment' (1992: 45). He goes on: 'the claim that an unregulated market in health care provides an incentive to doctors and hospitals to provide good service through competition becomes of doubtful validity … consumers will not "shop around" whenever they get ill, but will seek care from a supplier with whom they have built a long-term relationship' (1992: 45). Imperfect information and the inability to tell the difference between 'good treatment and bad treatment' (*ibid.*) mean that patients are extremely flawed consumers.

Related to the problem of imperfect information is the monopoly of provision that tends to result from it. Because patients are loyal to their health-care providers, this tends to mean hospitals and doctors do not compete with one another, and there is the potential, in economic theory at least, for them to raise their prices. Equally, supplier-induced demand can occur through doctors over-prescribing, especially where they are paid per item of treatment.

Turning to externalities, Le Grand defines this feature in health care as being when 'a third party who is not involved in the decision to consume (or produce) … is none the less affected by it, but receives no compensation or payment' (1992: 46). Externalities can be positive (benefits) or negative (costs). Communicable diseases create externalities, and so emphasize the importance of maintaining a high vaccination rate so that everyone in a population is protected.

In terms of market provision, externalities are important because where they exist to a significant extent, the 'market can no longer be relied upon to operate efficiently' (1992: 47). To continue with the example of vaccination, if, under a private market system, a charge were introduced for vaccination, it might mean that individuals would reason that the benefits they receive for being vaccinated might be less than the cost of receiving the vaccination – the private benefit would be less than the private cost. However, when social benefits are factored in, the benefits may well exceed the costs. What is socially the right thing to do might not correspond with what is individually the best decision – a tragedy of the commons situation. Le Grand presents a second example where hospital beds might be underprovided because, for a private provider of care, they are not profitable, as the private benefits of provision only, and not the social benefits, are taken into account. Market provision might therefore lead to underprovision.

Having worked through these analytical headings, Le Grand suggests that a market allocation of health care is unlikely to be fair or equitable (1992: 50).

Le Grand then moves on to his assessment of government policies of the time. In terms of regulation, he notes that consumers lack the information to judge the professional competence of doctors or hospital services, so this role has been taken up by governments. However, governments, in turn, have often delegated the regulation role to medical groups, leading to the danger of what economists call 'regulatory capture', where regulators rule in favour of the professional group they are meant to be controlling rather than in favour of, in the case of health care, patients.

In terms of provision, Le Grand suggests that the monopoly purchasing power of the government (acting as a monopsonist) has counteracted the monopoly power of the medical profession, and has, in the UK, limited the growth of high-technology medicine and managed to achieve some correction of geographic inequalities. However, he suggests, problems have come along with this:

> The state provider acting as a monopoly has limited the potential for competition and allowed the potential for inefficiencies to appear, and that the patterns of services that developed will probably depend more on the power of individual doctors and bureaucrats than on relative costs and benefits. (1992: 55–6)

After a discussion of subsidies in health care, Le Grand then briefly discusses the internal market introduced by the Conservatives in 1989. He suggests a number of problems. First, producers must be able to expand capacity quickly in order to meet additional demand, but also contract, and neither an expansion nor a reduction is politically likely to be achieved. Second, an absence of data on the quality of outcomes 'may make the system cost driven' (1992: 61). This leads to a potential clash between affordability and quality. Finally, the health-care reforms had not addressed the problem that the UK health-care system was underfinanced, and so they had not dealt with a significant problem facing the system as a whole.

In all then, Le Grand's analysis in 1992 seems pessimistic about the prospects for using a market effectively in health care. He is concerned that a public monopoly might result in inefficient care being provided, but at the same time is suggesting that the NHS as a whole is under-resourced. He acknowledges a range of problems with a market place for health, derived mostly from an economic analysis of market inefficiencies that might result.

The other invisible hand (2007)

By 2007, Le Grand presents a different analysis. He suggests that, 'in general, the choice-and-competition model for delivering public services is indeed an effective instrument for improving the quality, efficiency, responsiveness and equity of those services – especially when compared with the alternatives' (2007: 95). He goes on to say that critics of the model have suggested that markets can only work in certain conditions (largely those which Le Grand suggested fifteen years earlier).

Le Grand begins with a discussion of 'ends and means', noting that the 'principal problems of interpretation arise in the case of quality and equity' (2007: 96). He defines equity in terms of 'the extent to which equal treatment for equal need is observed' (2007: 97), and presents a critique of publicly funded health care in terms of meeting this definition.

Le Grand suggests that where patients are dissatisfied with the quality of treatment they are getting, they have only a limited range of options available: they can switch to private provision if they can afford it; or they can complain, which depends upon the goodwill (or knightliness) of the person to whom they are complaining. However, a knavish doctor or manager may have no incentive to respond, and complaint, being based on voice, favours the 'self-confident and articulate middle classes' (2007: 98). He then contrasts this with a world where choice and competition are the norm; patients who do not like the service they are receiving move instead to another provider 'who can provide them with better service' (*ibid.*), and if money follows the patient, 'then the hospital or practice that provides the best service will gain resources; that which provides the inferior service will lose' (*ibid.*).

Le Grand accepts there are some situations where choice might not be possible, but that 'the number of conditions where choice is impossible or unwanted should not be exaggerated' (2007: 99). Having outlined a theoretical model of how choice should work, he then moves on to its application in practice.

Presenting evidence from US research from Carol Propper, Le Grand suggests that 'competition in the United States with fixed prices both reduced costs and increased quality ... especially in markets where HMO penetration was high ... the effect of competition was to give more appropriate treatment, with sick patients in less competitive markets receiving less intensive treatment with worse health outcomes than they did in more competitive ones' (2007: 101). He presents further evidence that 'when patients deliberately choose not to go to their local medical facility for treatment but choose to go further afield, their health outcomes are better' (*ibid.*), and going further, that 'exercising choice is good for one's health: that the sense of control that choice gives has a powerful effect on individuals' ability to respond to treatment and their speed of recovery' (2007: 102).

Le Grand then brings in some problems observed in the US system, particularly cream-skimming, and the problem he observed fifteen years previously, that 'the users and purchasers of health care find it difficult properly to assess quality and hence to observe quality reduction' (2007: 102) – leaving the reader a little unclear as to how the market is therefore meant to work. If prices were fixed in the USA, and quality difficult to measure, how were the improvements he suggests above achieved? Moreover, he admits that 'we must be careful not to make too simplistic a comparison between the US health system and those of other countries' (2007: 100).

In terms of UK evidence, Le Grand refers the reader to an earlier review he led, suggesting that, despite an increase in transaction costs that occurred during the internal market reforms in the 1990s, efficiency appeared to rise, and that after the claimed abolition of the market by Labour in 1997, efficiency appeared to fall (2007: 103). He suggests that cream-skimming did not appear, and that GP fundholders did achieve a better deal for their patients. He does not deal with the problem that inequities between fundholding and non-fundholding practices must therefore have been created, and that patients must not have understood they stood to gain by joining a fundholding practice, emphasizing a continuing problem with information he was happy to suggest was commonplace fifteen years earlier.

Overall, Le Grand suggests that the 1990s internal market produced relatively small measurable changes, because 'competition in the market was limited, and this in turn may have been because some of the essential conditions for the market to operate were not fulfilled ... the incentives for the market players were too weak and the constraints imposed by central government were too strong' (2007: 104–5).

Le Grand then moves on to discuss evidence from the choice experiments tried out in London, where those who had waited over six months for treatment were offered it in an alternative hospital, with patients being given an adviser and help with transport costs. Take-up, Le Grand correctly suggests, was high (about two-thirds), with no difference in take-up between different socio-economic groups except that the unemployed took up the offer of choice less frequently than the employed, and that significant impacts upon waiting times were achieved. However, Le Grand does not quite present the full picture here – choice in the rest of the country is very different to the pilot choice programme in London. The rest of the country has far less dense provision, and so less potential for competition, and patient choice advisers have not appeared widely. Equally, choice is not only offered to long waiters, but to everyone at the time of referral, and so a significant difference in terms of the perception of wait is in place. Finally, the offer of paying for transport costs is far less likely to be present.

Le Grand then draws lessons from his evidence. First, he suggests that competition must be real – that alternative providers must be available. He confronts the argument that London cannot be regarded as representative of the rest of the country by pointing to a study showing that 92 per cent of the country had two or more acute trusts within sixty minutes travelling time by car. However, two or more trusts hardly seems to count as being much choice: in economists' terms, this is an oligopoly. Second, the question must be asked as to whether patients are really willing to travel sixty minutes to get treatment from an alternative provider to the one closer to them. Le Grand rightly points out that the British population as a whole is remarkably urbanized, and that 'the rural tail must not wag the urban dog' (2007: 107), but one has to wonder what has happened to the difficulties he pointed out in his earlier work. Where have the information asymmetries between doctors and patients, and the patient choice inertia he noted fifteen years previously, gone?

Equally, this analysis ignores that fact that provider competition is unevenly distributed in terms of treatment. Relatively simple surgery such as hip and knee replacements can be carried out by treatment centres, but whether it is necessary or desirable for them to be carrying out cancer care is another question. The private sector is incentivized to enter markets where it can make money, so areas of care that require treatment of uncertain duration or cost are more likely to remain in public provision. In theory, price (tariff, in contemporary NHS parlance) levels can be set to try and encourage private entry into every area of care, but the uncertainty attached to patients with long-term conditions, especially at time of diagnosis, will tend to mean that public provision will always be necessary for them. This is likely to lead to public providers having to provide treatments of uncertain cost and complexity, whereas the private sector competes only in areas where it can see a calculable return. Public organizations therefore have to compete on unfair terms – they are left with all the difficult cases.

Le Grand goes on to suggest ways of increasing competition further, advocating help with transport costs for the poor so that they are able to exercise choice. However, this last point again seems to ignore the problem that, whereas most people are prepared prospectively to say that they would like more choice about health care, when they are ill, especially with more serious conditions, this declines significantly. Research reports that 65 per cent of people say they would want to choose their treatment if they got cancer but only 12 per cent of actual cancer patients said they wanted the same freedom (Schwartz 2004). We do not have enough research yet exploring the conditions for which patients would like choices compared to those where they wouldn't, and how far they are prepared to travel in practice (rather than theoretically) in order not to go to their local health-care provider. Le Grand in 2007 seems to be making very different assumptions about patients than in 1992.

In terms of the benefits of market entrance, Le Grand presents evidence from manufacturing plants between 1980 and 1992 that shows an increase in productivity coming from new entrants, but admits that this may not be transferable to health care. He also suggests that independent treatment centres, since entering the NHS, have been significantly more productive, with shorter lengths of stay and more innovative practice, but emphasizes that it is early days in terms of the data. He does not refer to the other side of the argument, that independent treatment centre patients have often been self-selecting in terms of being among the most healthy and able patients, and also does not deal with the barrage of criticisms that have been made against them in terms of the quality of care they have offered.

In terms of market exit, Le Grand presents several pages detailing the problems of allowing institutions in public markets to fail, but suggests that a 'rule driven' system needs to be introduced that does not allow political interference with particular 'triggers' in place, such as deficits exceeding 3 per cent of income for two consecutive years, allowing closure and exit to proceed. This suggestion seems to ignore the problem that the reason why political interference occurs in health organizations is often because a large number of the public demand it. The same public Le Grand is characterizing as sophisticated and careful decision-makers can be ignored when they collectively demand that their local hospital remain open. This seems an odd logic.

Le Grand then moves on to a second significant lesson; that choice must be informed. He acknowledges that 'there is little evidence that, when presented with information about, for instance, the quality of outcomes by individual surgeons, patients actually use that information to make appropriate judgements' (2007: 117–18). However, Le Grand suggests that even if patients don't use this information, providers do use it to improve their performance, perhaps because of professional pride, and perhaps because of the threat of reputational damage. Further, Le Grand suggests that information can be made more accessible, and that the Patient Care Adviser role used in pilots in the UK might be extended, even if there is a danger that it would cost a great deal and might become another level of professionals between the patient and the service itself.

In sum, in terms of his analysis of health-care markets, Le Grand appears to be suggesting that patients don't really use health information at present (but they might if it were presented in a form they could understand), and that patient care advisers are necessary for choices to work.

Finally, Le Grand moves on to a long discussion of cream-skimming, and the potential dangers that a combination of patient choice and money following the patient might create. He suggests that there will be some negative impact on equity arising from patient choice enhancing cream-skimming effects. He then makes suggestions for how this might be avoided. He suggests that, where a patient has a complex condition that might fall outside of the usual price, a 'stop-loss' insurance scheme could be in place to remove potential discrimination against high-cost patients, but acknowledges a problem that hospitals would have no incentive to economize on treatment in such cases. An additional problem he does not point out is that hospitals would also have a strong incentive to get as many 'stop-loss' patients as possible in order to maximize their potential revenues.

Le Grand also suggests that admissions lists might be removed from hospitals completely so that they were required to take whichever patients were being referred to them. This is already happening in the 'choose and book' system, whereby patient appointments can be made to at least some consultant lists without patients first being assessed. This would, however, mean that patients would have to receive standardized appointment times with no attempt made to see more ill patients earlier or for longer, and would also mean that all appointments would potentially be on a first-come, first-served basis. While acknowledging that appointments should be booked as quickly as possible, it does seem odd to remove consultants from the decision about who should be treated first.

Finally, Le Grand suggests that tariffs might be weighted in terms of severity of condition (which is already happening, but gives hospitals the incentive to grade patients at the maximum severity, and for purchasers of care instead to claim they are at the minimum), and even that tariffs might be weighted according to a deprivation index so that those living in poorer areas attract higher resources. Le Grand concludes that 'choice-and-competition systems can achieve the ends of health-care policy. But they must be properly designed to as to meet the conditions for effectiveness' (2007: 126).

Discussion

The comparisons of Le Grand's most recent work with earlier periods suggest two main contrasts. While his broad economic approach remains unchanged, the detailed template of analysis and the attention given to individual elements has changed. There is continuity in that there is a principal–agent model of human agency in both periods. By 2007 the principal is far more driven, prepared to travel, and prepared to make use of health information presented to her, whereas in 1992 patients were far more risk-averse and loyal to local health provision. Equally, there is no acknowledgement that patient choice might be a negative phenomenon as well as a positive one, as Schwartz suggests, or that the severity of treatment might affect the willingness to choose. Equally, it is not clear how individual patients are to hold doctors to account in the principal–agent model where they do not understand clearly the nature of the service they are receiving. This was acknowledged as a significant difficulty in 1992, but seems to be missing from his analysis in 2007.

Externalities have just about disappeared from Le Grand's analysis between 1992 and 2007. He argues that most health care does not generate externalities – as Lipsey (2007: 176) comments, Le Grand does not explicitly reject externality arguments, but does not think them very important. Problems which were deemed significant in 1992, such as cream-skimming and asymmetric knowledge, appear to be less important and more soluble in 2007. Lipsey (2005, 2007) argues that public services have three characteristics that make them different from the type of commodities sold in supermarkets, making them inappropriate for the introduction of choice and competition: externalities, agency and information. Le Grand (2007: 57) replies that poor user information is a genuine problem for choice in health care and education – although no more so than for other methods of involving users of those services, but there is certainly very little discussion of agency problems in 2007.

Moreover, Le Grand has moved from the 'veneer of academic detachment' towards being more of a policy advocate. However, he finds difficulty in dealing with the problem that patients do not appear generally to understand the information put before them, never mind that they also may not want to choose in health care. The problem may be an interrelated one – the lack of understanding of how choices are to be made, when combined with the personal risk that may be implicit in taking responsibility for choice decisions, may mean they don't want the same choices that they may want in education, for example. Equally, we do not understand how far (if at all) patients are prepared to travel to make choice work – so any assumption of distance is fallacious.

Le Grand's role as government adviser meant that he became more concerned with 'incremental' rather than 'rational' policy analysis. Rather than starting with a blank piece of academic analysis (policies in an ideal world), he had to start 'from here', with the existing policy landscape, and consider ways of improving it. For example, he claims that incentives and opportunities for risk selection or cream-skimming exist in the current NHS and then asks whether the introduction of patient choice for elective surgery and other forms of non-emergency treatment makes things better or worse (2007: 123).

The second main change in Le Grand's work appears to be in terms of conclusions, and this has some parallels with Labour's change of mind on market mechanisms and choice. In 1997 Labour aimed to abolish the internal market in health care and ended the Assisted Places scheme in education and nursery vouchers (Powell 2007). While Le Grand has long had some reservations about bureaucratic allocation (Le Grand 1982; but see Powell 1995), he seems to have abandoned some of his earlier qualifications and caveats about quasi-markets to more fully support individual choice. As recently as 2003, in his comparison of education and health care, he presented parents as active agents, but in health care characterized GPs in this role suggesting that 'this in part seems to be a sensible reflection of the differences between the two cases in the extent of system and individual failure' as 'the information available to users and their capacity properly to process that information is arguably less in the case of health care than education. Hence appointing an informed agent to make choices on behalf of users seems more appropriate for health care', but 'it is important that users can choose their agent: hence the recommendation ... that patients should be able to choose their primary-care trust' (2003: 117–18). Since 2003 Le Grand has seemed to present an extremely positive interpretation of the evidence on topics such as the London Patient Choice and social care direct budgets. Has he come to accentuate the positive and eliminate (or downplay) the negative, or are the critics too pessimistic?

Le Grand's position seems to have changed over time. While he has long been a supporter of some quasi-market reforms such as GP fundholding – with important caveats and qualifications (Glennerster and Le Grand 1995), his support for choice and competition now appears broader and deeper. There are several possible reasons for this change. Perhaps Le Grand has either been convinced by new evidence (in a similar way to former Secretary of State Alan Milburn, for example), or the current Labour government's reforms have addressed some of the problems of the previous Conservative government's market, or the public has become more consumerist in orientation (cf. Secretary of State for Health 2000). However, no matter how consumerist the public's orientation in other areas of their life, when it comes to health care, as a whole they seem remarkably unwilling to act upon information that is available to them. We are all growing more obese and apparently engaging in more unhealthy activities in other aspects of our life, such as drinking and drug-taking, despite the mass of evidence saying how bad for us all this is. Le Grand has intervened in public health areas himself, calling for more incentives to be put in place for people to adopt healthier lifestyles, but the fact that this is necessary suggests that the public still do not put a premium on health information, and that if they are unwilling or unable to respond appropriately to public health information, there is little evidence to suggest that they will respond appropriately to information about health choices between local care providers.

Conclusion: The Other Julian Le Grand?

The comparisons of Le Grand's most recent work with earlier periods suggest two main contrasts in terms of approach and conclusions. We also believe that markets can work in some areas of social policy (see, for example, Greener 2008); however, we tend in general to be more sceptical (cf. Lipsey 2005, 2007) and more contextual: more choice and competition might be possible in primary education than in rail travel (Greener 2008).

Le Grand is among our most important writers on social policy. His arguments in favour of choice and competition present an important challenge to much of the social policy orthodoxy. Lipsey (2007: 175) asserts that the opponents of choice in public services often use bad arguments. We hope that, in focusing on Le Grand's own analytical template, we have contributed to this important debate. We continue to admire the range and scope of his work, and recognize entirely his right to present his views as he wishes. However, we would urge him not to lose sight of his earlier work, and of the powerful critiques of market-based reforms that it offers. In advocating *The Other Invisible Hand*, we hope he will not forget the earlier, other Le Grand.

References

Bartlett, W., Roberts, J. and Le Grand, J. (eds) (1998), *A Revolution in Social Policy*, Bristol: Policy Press.

Fabian Society (2000), *Paying for Progress: Report of the Commission on Taxation and Citizenship*, London: Fabian Society.

Glennerster, H. and Le Grand, J. (1995), The development of quasi-markets in welfare provision in the United Kingdom, *International Journal of Health Services*, 25: 203–18.

Greener, I. (2008), Markets in the public sector: when do they work, and what do we do when they don't? *Policy and Politics*, 36, 1: 93–108.

Institute for Public Policy Research (IPPR) (2001), *Building Better Partnerships*, The Final Report of the Commission on Public Private Partnerships, London: IPPR.

Le Grand, J. (1982), *The Strategy of Equality*, London: Allen and Unwin.

Le Grand, J. (1991), Tales from the British National Health Service: Competition, Cooperation or Control? *Health Affairs*, 18: 27–37.

Le Grand, J. (1997), Knights, knaves or pawns? Human behaviour and social policy, *Journal of Social Policy*, 26: 149–69.

Le Grand, J. (2002), The Labour Government and the National Health Service, *Oxford Review of Economic Policy*, 18: 137–57.

Le Grand, J. (2003), *Motivation, Agency and Public Policy: Of Knights and Knaves, Pawns and Queens*, Oxford: Oxford University Press.

Le Grand, J. (ed.) (2007), *The Other Invisible Hand: Delivering Public Services through Choice and Competition*, Princeton, NJ: Princeton University Press.

Le Grand, J. and Bartlett, W. (eds) (1993), *Quasi-Markets and Social Policy*, Basingstoke: Macmillan.

Le Grand, J. and Robinson, R. (1976), *The Economics of Social Problems*, London: Macmillan.

Le Grand, J., Propper, C. and Robinson, R. (1992), *The Economics of Social Problems*, 3rd edn, London: Palgrave Macmillan.

Le Grand, J., Mays, N. and Mulligan, J.-A. (eds) (1998), *Learning from the NHS Internal Market*, London: King's Fund.

Lipsey, D. (2005), Too much choice, *Prospect*, 117 (December): 26–9.

Lipsey, D. (2007), A sceptic's perspective. In J. Le Grand (ed.), *The Other Invisible Hand*, Princeton, NJ: Princeton University Press, pp. 174–9.

Powell, M. (1995), The strategy of equality revisited, *Journal of Social Policy*, 24, 2: 163–85.

Powell, M. (2003), Quasi-markets in British health policy: a longue durée perspective, *Social Policy & Administration*, 37, 7: 725–41.

Powell, M. (ed.) (2007), *Understanding the Mixed Economy of Welfare*, Bristol: Policy Press.

Roberts, J., Le Grand, J. and Bartlett, W. (1998), Conclusion: lessons from experience of quasi-markets in the 1990s. In W. Bartlett, J. Roberts and J. Le Grand (eds), *A Revolution in Social Policy*, Bristol: Policy Press, pp. 275–90.

Schwartz, B. (2004), *The Paradox of Choice: Why Less is More*, New York: HarperCollins.

Secretary of State for Health (2000), *The NHS Plan*, London: Stationery Office.

3
Exit, Voice and Quality in the English Education Sector
Deborah Wilson

Introduction

The use of choice as a mechanism to improve public service delivery is now well established in the UK. Current policy discourse additionally considers voice as a further, user-driven mechanism. Moreover, choice and voice are considered to be complementary, as these quotes from a recent Prime Minister's Strategy Unit discussion article illustrate: 'Choice and voice should complement each other … Bottom-up pressure through choice and voice can … give everyone, including the disadvantaged, better quality services' (PMSU 2006: 10). This discourse about choice and voice working together to improve quality can be traced back to Hirschman (1970), who argues that exit (choice) and voice are two consumer responses to deterioration in the quality of a firm's product or service.[1] These provide signals to the firm, which responds by improving quality, thereby creating a self-correcting mechanism via which quality standards are maintained. Hirschman argues that different combinations of exit and/or voice are suitable in different settings, depending on which signal(s) the firm is most responsive to.

Bottom–up pressure is just one of four elements of the UK government framework for improving quality in public service delivery (PMSU 2006). The model of public service reform also incorporates top–down performance management, competition/contestability, and increasing the capability and capacity of public servants. It is recognized that this general model needs to be tailored to each service; in particular, 'The appropriate mix of top–down pressure, competition and bottom–up choice and voice will therefore vary from case to case' (PMSU 2006: 11).

The current English education system provides one clear example of these different elements in operation.[2] Parental choice is emphasized as a key driver to improve quality, with parents also encouraged to make their voices heard (via parent councils and parent governorships, for example). Parental choice is informed by school performance tables and Ofsted reports, which form part of the 'top–down' performance management regime in which schools have targets based on published student outcomes. Schools in England compete for pupils in order to maintain numbers and therefore levels of funding, and new entry into the market – by Academies, for example – is being encouraged. The government's commitment to improving the capability and capacity of the education sector workforce can be illustrated by the formation of the Training and Development Agency for Schools (TDA) in September 2005.[3] The aim is for all these elements to combine to create a 'self-improving system', providing high-quality education for all pupils.

In this chapter I investigate one aspect of this general reform programme in the context of education. Specifically, I scrutinize the assumption that choice (exit) and voice do complement each other in creating user-driven incentives to increase the quality of education provision for all. I do this by going back to Hirschman's original thesis, focusing in particular on the implications of the definitions of 'quality' put forward by him. I apply his analysis to the English education context and show that, while the current policy discourse evokes the language of Hirschman, it doesn't follow through on the actual implications of his analysis. In particular, I argue that in the current system, choice and voice may complement each other for only a subset of consumers.

Hirschman's Exit, Voice, Loyalty and Quality

Hirschman (1970) argues that a process of decline in the quality of a firm's output (for whatever reason) activates certain consumer responses, which in turn act as endogenous forces of recovery, thereby reversing the initial decline in quality. This is a self-correction mechanism, whereby the very process of decline activates certain counterforces and hence generates its own cure. He distinguishes two contrasting consumer responses – exit and voice. Exit is 'the sort of mechanism economics thrives on' (1970: 15). It is neat, impersonal and indirect: subsequent recovery by the firm comes via the market. Voice, by contrast, is more 'messy', more personal and more direct, and can cover anything from personal complaint to collective action. Hirschman's particular interest is how, and under what circumstances, exit and voice may combine to best rectify or reverse a (relative or absolute) decline in quality of a firm's product or service:

> how a typical market mechanism and a typical non-market, political mechanism work side by side, possibly in harmony and mutual support, possibly also in such a fashion that one gets into the other's way and undercuts its effectiveness. (Hirschman 1970: 18)

To be effective, he argues, the signal used – exit or voice – should correspond with that to which the organization is responsive, which in turn depends on the particular service/product and/or organization being considered.[4] He identifies a particular problem, however: that over-emphasis on less costly exit may reduce investment in (may 'atrophy') voice, even in circumstances when voice may be the most effective mechanism for improving quality. This is because those consumers who care most about quality – and who would be the most active agents of voice – are for that very reason those most likely to exit first when faced with a decline in that quality. If the firm is more responsive to voice, this will make the self-correction mechanism less effective at restoring levels of quality. Hirschman recognizes a tension between exit and voice: consumers' willingness to develop and use the voice mechanism is reduced by exit, but the presence of an exit option increases the effectiveness of voice.

One way in which exit, particularly by quality-sensitive consumers, may be delayed is through what Hirschman calls loyalty: 'The importance of loyalty … is that it can neutralize within certain limits the tendency of the most quality-conscious customers or members to be the first to exit' (1970: 79). Loyalty is psychological, not behavioural (Dowding *et al*. 2000), and can be understood in terms of a generalized barrier to exit which may be directly imposed or internally generated. Hirschman argues that staying within a declining organization may in fact be rational if, by exiting, the quality of the organization further declines, *and* the consumer cares about the quality of the organization even after s/he has left it.[5] This in turn implies that s/he does not fully exit ('voice from within' compared to 'voice from without'). Hirschman introduces the term 'quality-maker' to describe that situation where a consumer's exit causes quality to further decline, a term to which I shall refer in my application of his analysis to the education context.[6]

Hirschman (1970) identifies two scenarios with regard to quality. The majority of his analysis draws on the assumption that a change in quality is felt in the same direction by all consumers: individuals may be differentially sensitive to such a change, but all agree that it is either a decline or an improvement. In the analysis that follows, I will additionally use the term 'unidimensional' quality to describe this scenario: quality can improve or decline along only one dimension, and, as with Hirschman, individuals all agree on the direction of change along that dimension. Hirschman more briefly considers the case when a change in quality is felt in different directions by different consumers: individuals may disagree on whether an increase in the level of a particular service is a good or a bad thing depending on their political affiliations, for example. I introduce the term 'multidimensional' quality to describe this scenario, where the preferences of consumers differ across alternative dimensions and hence they may disagree whether changes along any one dimension represent a decline or improvement in quality. Hirschman's quality distinction parallels that between vertical and horizontal product differentiation in the economics literature (Gaynor 2006). With vertical product differentiation ('product quality'), all consumers have the same preferences and so agree that some products are better than others. With horizontal product differentiation ('product variety'), consumers can have differing preferences and thus some may like one product while others prefer another. In the analysis that follows I will use these terms interchangeably. Crucially, Hirschman shows that the operation of exit and/or voice yields different outcomes depending on which concept of quality is relevant. I briefly describe the relevant features of the English education sector before applying Hirschman's concepts of quality to that context and investigating the resultant predicted outcomes.

The English Education Sector

Parental choice of school has been a feature of the English education system since 1989. This is 'generalised but differential' choice (Burgess *et al.* 2007): all parents express a choice of the preferred school for their child, but the extent to which that preference is realized varies across the country (see Burgess *et al.* 2006, for a quantitative analysis of the outcomes of the current system). The choices – or preferences – are informed by in-depth Ofsted reports on individual schools, plus annually published school performance (league) tables. Until 2002 the published performance measures provided summary informa-tion on raw test scores – the proportion of pupils gaining at least five 'good' GCSE passes (5A*–C), for example. Currently these raw outcome measures are still published, but now along with information on the 'contextual value added' (CVA) provided by the school (Wilson and Piebalga 2008). CVA aims to provide a better measure of the actual impact of the school on pupil progress, i.e. its effectiveness, by accounting for factors that are known to impact on pupil attainment but which are outside the school's control. The aim is that parental choice acts as a driver for schools to improve 'quality'; I return to what that means below.

Alongside choice, parents are encouraged to exercise voice in the education system in a number of ways: at an individual level via the personalization of the curriculum agenda (PMSU 2006; Strategy Unit 2008) as well as getting involved in the running of the school through becoming a parent governor or a member of the parent-teacher association (PTA). Parents are also able to make complaints about the education their child is receiving, although in practice it may be difficult for parents to do this (Vincent and Martin 2002).[7] There are also options for collective voice in this system, through parent councils, for example, as well as parents acting together to get a new school built, or trying to stop an existing school being closed.

I distinguish three key players or agents in this education 'market'. First are the parents, who are the 'consumers' of education, able to show their concern about quality by exercising choice and/or voice.[8] Second are the schools, which need to be responsive to such signals in order that quality might improve. Finally, the government is responsible for the top–down system of performance management, which creates particular incentives for schools via, for example, the targets they face, and within which the system of parental choice operates (Wilson *et al.* 2006).

So what is 'quality' in this context? As Le Grand (2007) discusses, there are many possible meanings of quality in the context of public services. He dis-tinguishes four alternative means by which quality can be defined: inputs, process, outputs, and outcomes. While 'raising the overall quality of a school system is perhaps the principal objective of any such educational policy' (2007: 64), in practice most empirical attention is usually focused on measuring quality through educational inputs, and/or on one interpretation of out-comes: the standards of achievement as measured by test results. This out-comes interpretation of quality links to the definitions of quality I employ in this chapter, informed by the distinctions made by Hirschman. Specifically,

I distinguish quality as effectiveness, or 'value added', from quality as the basis for parental choice.

First, quality as effectiveness, or 'value added'. I argue that this is closest to the government aim of improving actual school performance – the impact schools have on the progress of all their pupils. I also argue that this corresponds to Hirschman's notion of a change in quality being felt in the same direction by all consumers (what I call unidimensional quality), i.e. that all consumers see an increase in school effectiveness as an improvement. As Le Grand (2007) states, however, the emphasis has not been on value-added performance measures; rather it has been on outcomes as measured by test results and proxied, for example, by the 5A*–C performance measure. This is still the basis for the headline figures in league tables; the key measures of 'quality' used both in the top–down performance management regime and to inform bottom–up parental choice. How does this link with Hirschman's analysis? Any measure of raw output includes information on the pupils as well as on the school performance; on its composition as well as its effectiveness. In other words, such measures include the pupil as an input as well as an output to the education production process: for example, high-ability pupils will produce high scores on raw output measures, all other things being equal. This links directly to Hirschman's concept of a quality-maker.

Second, quality as the basis for parental choice. While academic standards are important to parents (Coldron and Boulton 1991; West and Pennell 1999), there is evidence to suggest that parents do not choose their preferred school solely on the basis of league table information (test scores or value added). Rothstein (2004), for example, finds that school effectiveness is not a primary determinant of parental decisions,[9] while Reay and Lucey (2003) find that it is how similar children perform at a school that matters more than overall school averages. Butler and Robson's (2003) study shows that performance tables are not the sole arbiter of the parental choice decision, and that the ethos of the school also matters. Ball *et al.* (1995) similarly discuss the importance of the 'expressive order' of a school. School composition is a further dimension that matters to parents, possibly in different ways. Ball and Vincent (1998) argue that many parents feel strongly that it is important to keep their child with children from the same social and/or ethnic group, while Jellison Holme's (2002) US study suggests that the most coveted schools for privileged parents are those without low-income or minority ethnic students. Several studies show how parental preferences vary by income, ethnicity and/or socio-economic background (see, for example, Gerwitz *et al.* 1995; Hastings *et al.* 2005; Weekes-Bernard 2007). It is sometimes not clear whether a parent's stated preference represents choice or constraint (Reay and Lucey 2003); the importance of the location of the school provides one example of this. The key point from this for the current analysis is that parents have different preferences across the various aspects of school quality, which means that individuals may disagree whether changes in specific dimensions of this quality are a good or a bad thing. This links with my multidimensional concept of quality.

Applying Hirschman's Concepts of Quality to the Education Context

A change in quality is felt in the same direction by all: unidimensional quality

The assumption that a change in quality is felt in the same direction by all consumers underlies much of Hirschman's analysis. In this case, consumers agree on whether a change is an improvement or a decline in quality, but they may be differentially sensitive to such change. If quality declines, exit and voice are complementary in the sense that they both work to improve quality, as long as the signal used is that to which the organization is responsive. There are spill-overs or externalities between alert and inalert consumers: the latter benefit from the quality improvement brought about by the exit or voice of the former precisely because they all see it as an improvement.

These results have parallels with the theoretical predictions from the economics literature on vertical product differentiation when prices are regulated (Gaynor 2006). If prices are regulated, firms compete for consumers on non-price dimensions. Under the assumption of vertical product differentiation, competition unambiguously increases quality, although not necessarily to the social welfare-maximizing level. If voice works in the same direction as exit, the introduction of voice should not alter this broad finding: an increase in exit and/or voice leads to an increase in 'product quality' if prices are regulated.

As discussed above, however, the presence of exit may reduce investment in voice: exit may atrophy voice. The most quality-sensitive, and therefore the potentially most vocal, are likely to be the first to exit, leaving behind less vocal consumers. This is a problem if the organization is more responsive to voice, as the signal it needs to improve quality will be weaker and the self-correction mechanism therefore less effective.

So if a quality change is felt in the same direction by all consumers, Hirschman argues that exit and voice are complementary and there are spill-overs between alert and inalert consumers, but there is the potential for overemphasis on exit even when the firm is more responsive to voice, which may prevent or delay recovery.

Application to the English education sector. Consider quality as school effectiveness, or value added, an improvement which, I argue, is felt as such by all consumers.[10] In this case, the Hirschman thesis suggests that exit and voice will indeed be complementary; that both these user-driven mechanisms will work together to provide signals to the schools to improve their effectiveness. The actions of the alert will cause spill-overs for the inalert consumers, as all benefit from the agreed-upon improvement. This sounds very much like the 'rising tide that raises all boats' scenario of Hoxby (2003), which reflects the result from the economics literature that 'product quality' increases with competition.

But what about the problem of exit atrophying voice? Hirschman argues that the possibility of exit reduces investment in voice, and that the most vocal exit first which leaves less scope for effective voice. This is not a problem, however, if schools are more responsive to the exit signal than to voice. The degree of responsiveness of schools to different user signals is determined by the incentives they face, i.e. by the design of the performance management regime within which choice and voice operate (Paul 1992). There is therefore a fundamental link between the bottom–up and top–down elements of the system. The current system in England, in which school funding relies directly on pupil numbers, is one in which school incentives are based more on choice than on voice, so atrophy should not be a problem: the top–down perform-ance management system creates the incentive for schools to respond to the choice signal. One implication of this, however, is that if policy-makers are attempting to introduce more options for voice as an additional user-driven mechanism alongside choice, they need also to create the incentives for schools to respond to that signal, and to respond by improving their effectiveness.[11]

So if all the key players are (only) interested in quality as value added or effectiveness, the Hirschman analysis concurs with current policy discourse in predicting that choice and voice should complement one another in improving quality for all. The design of the performance management system is central to the relative degree of responsiveness of schools to the two signals.

A change in quality is felt in different directions by different consumers: quality is 'multidimensional'

The evidence suggests, however, that parents are not interested only in the measures of school performance that are published in league tables (value added or raw test scores). Parents take account of a much broader, more multidimensional view of quality when choosing the preferred school(s) for their children. Moreover, different aspects of the school environment matter to varying degrees across parents. Again, we turn to Hirschman and then apply his analysis to the education context.

Hirschman considers the case when a change in quality is not appreciated as such by all consumers, i.e. when consumers have a differential appreciation of the same quality change. He gives the example of different political affiliations leading to differing views regarding changes in local government spending. I argue that we can similarly think in terms of quality being multi-dimensional: a change in quality along one dimension may be appreciated by some but not by others. In such a scenario, Hirschman argues, organiza-tions have the possibility of changing quality in such a way as to please some while displeasing others. Which route will they take? To whom will they respond?

It proves useful to first consider the predictions from the theoretical eco-nomics literature. The relevant scenario is still one of regulated prices, but now with horizontal product differentiation ('product variety'). In a recent review of this area, however, Gaynor (2006) does not consider this scenario. He focuses solely on vertical product differentiation because 'it is well known that firms will pursue minimal product variety in the absence of price com-petition' (2006: 9). This result comes originally from Hotelling (1929), who

Deborah Wilson

showed that, under certain conditions, it is rational for firms to make their products as similar as possible. In particular, this result depends on the assumption of zero elasticity of demand for the firms' products along the linear market. Under this assumption, consumers will continue to buy the product from their nearest firm, regardless of how near it is. The incentive for the two profit-maximising firms is therefore to locate at the centre, i.e. produce the same product, and thus capture half the market.

As Hirschman (1970) points out, however, horizontal product differentiation with regulated prices is a common empirical reality.[12] One explanation may come from relaxing the assumption that demand is inelastic. If demand is elastic each firm would lose customers at its own end of the market as it moved towards the centre, and this provides the incentive for firms to maintain some degree of product differentiation (to stay away from the centre). An alternative explanation offered by Hirschman involves voice. As he states (1970: 70, italics in original): 'inelastic demand at the extremes of the linear market can spell considerable influence *via voice*'. Firms faced with both exit and voice signals may need to trade off profit maximization with discontent minimization, which may provide an incentive not to cluster at the centre of the linear market.

There are no specific predictions, however, arising from the Hirschman analysis regarding the outcomes with horizontal product differentiation and regulated prices in the presence of both exit and voice. Rather, Hirschman discusses in general terms the 'quality path' of the organization, and how this path depends on its responsiveness to exit and/or voice. For example, if it is more responsive to exit than voice, the organization is more likely to correct deviations from normal quality that are 'obnoxious' to its exit-prone customers. This may not be seen as an improvement by its vocal customers. Alternatively, if the organization is more responsive to voice, it may work to minimize discontent among its vocal customers by changing quality in ways that are not appreciated by those who are exit-prone. The quality path of the organization can therefore be predicted in different contexts, or under different assumptions regarding the relative responsiveness of the organization to the different signals. A key point for the purposes of the current analysis is that, if quality is multidimensional, exit and voice do not necessarily complement each other because exit-prone and more vocal consumers may view the same change in quality differently from one another. Moreover, there will be no spill-overs between alert or inalert consumers if they value different aspects of quality. Spill-overs may be possible in a multidimensional quality setting, but only if alert and inalert similarly value quality changes along the same dimension. They are no longer guaranteed.

Application to the English education sector. The notion of multidimensional quality seems in tune with the actual basis for choice of parents. As discussed above, the evidence suggests that the basis for choice is indeed multidimensional; that parents have different preferences across different dimensions of school 'quality': test scores, school composition, ethos, 'expressive order', location. In this case the Hirschman analysis predicts that there is no guarantee that choice and voice will complement each other, nor that there will be spill-overs

40

between alert and inalert consumers if they value different aspects of quality. There is no longer any guarantee of that 'rising tide'.

Can we say anything about the likely outcome, about the 'quality path' schools have the incentive to take in this case? I argue that the notion of the pupil as a quality-maker, and the fact that a centrally published performance measure of quality incorporates this, proves useful in predicting the outcome. While measures of (contextual) value added are now routinely published in the secondary school league tables, it is still the performance measures based on raw test scores that continue to provide the headline figures (Wilson and Piebalga 2008). The notion of consumers as quality-makers proves relevant to these 'headline' measures of quality. More generally, any measure of educational outcomes which does not explicitly account for input includes some notion of the pupil as a quality-maker.[13]

These raw output measures have been – and continue to be – the key indicator in the English school league tables. School rankings in the league tables matter to all key players in the education system (Wilson et al. 2006). Schools have the incentive to care about outcomes as measured by these summary indicators of raw test scores and therefore have the incentive to care about – to respond to signals from – pupils of high ability whose exit would reduce (or entry would enhance) quality as measured by such indicators, which directly relates to Hirschman's notion of consumer as a quality-maker. Specifically, they have the incentive to respond to the parents of high-ability children. Given the positive association between income and attainment, these are going to be, broadly speaking, middle-class parents. In the education context, the middle-class parents are likely to be the most exit-prone *and* the most vocal (Le Grand 2007). Contrary to Hirschman, therefore, there may not be a conflict between responding to (the threat of) exit or responding to voice in the multidimensional quality setting. Instead, schools currently have the incentive to respond to *either* signal from the parents whose children will boost (measured) quality. And this incentive comes from the design of the performance management (PM) system and, in particular, the importance of performance measures that incorporate pupils as quality-makers.

So choice and voice do complement each other, even though quality is multi-dimensional, *but* only for one type of consumer. And schools have the incentive to focus on the elements of quality preferred by that type of consumer. This provides one way of thinking about how to predict the resultant quality path followed by the school. For example, one aspect or dimension of quality which the school may subsequently have the incentive to change is composition. This provides potential links with the debates on (covert) selection by schools (Le Grand 2007). There has been recent evidence that some schools in England have being breaking admissions laws in ways which, according to Schools Minister Jim Knight, penalized poorer families.[14] Similarly, a recent government inquiry found that 17 per cent of the 570 secondary schools checked in three local authorities were breaking the admissions rules, for example by asking parents banned questions about marital status and financial background, or by not giving due priority to children in care or with special needs.[15]

The way in which 'quality' is measured, and the information subsequently published, thus provides a central link between the top–down and bottom–up elements of reform; between the incentives created by the former and the information on which parents at least partly base their choice.

Conclusion

The purpose of this chapter was to go back to the original Hirschman (1970) thesis to relate the policy discourse of choice and voice to his exit–voice distinction. In particular, I scrutinized the assumption that choice and voice complement each other to increase the quality of education provision for all. A careful analysis of Hirschman's arguments shows that the outcomes of such user-driven mechanisms fundamentally depend on how quality is defined. Applying his findings to the English education sector suggests the following. If we think of quality as school effectiveness or value added, a change in that quality is felt in the same direction by all. The use of choice and/or voice by alert consumers improves quality for all, provided schools are responsive to the signal(s) employed. This is no longer necessarily the case if we think in terms of a multi-dimensional concept of quality. If the most exit-prone and the most vocal are different consumers, choice and voice may work in different directions. If, however, the same consumers are most exit-prone *and* most vocal, choice and voice may complement each other to improve quality along the dimension valued (possibly only) by that group. I argue that the latter is more likely to be the case in the education context; that it is the middle-class parents who are seen as most likely to exercise both choice and voice. The question then is whether schools have the incentive to respond to either signal from this subset of parents. I argue that they do so, given the incentives created by the league tables and in particular the fact that the headline figures, based on raw test scores, incorporate the notion of the pupil as quality-maker. This suggests that the current UK policy discourse may be misleading in the education context: choice and voice can work together to improve quality, but maybe only for a subset of consumers. The discourse evokes the language of Hirschman but not the actual implications of his analysis.

This analysis further shows that these alternative concepts of 'quality' provide a useful framework for thinking about potential outcomes from combinations of the bottom–up and top–down elements of reform across different areas of public service delivery. These different concepts will be applicable in varying degrees across these different areas. Following from this, the current analysis represents a starting point for a broader research programme, both with regard to exit/voice in different public services, and with regard to the other elements of the reform programme (trust, capability, for example). This analysis also highlights the need for more empirical evidence on the basis for parental choice of school; on the correlations – positive and/or negative – between the different dimensions of school quality and, in particular, between the preferences of different parents across those dimensions. This will inform the extent to which schools responding to one group of consumers (here, for example, the middle-class parents) are also improving quality along the dimensions valued by other groups, which will in turn provide evidence on the extent to which spill-overs may in fact be possible within a multidimensional quality setting.

My analysis has further implications for policy. First, it provides a further argument against the publication of school performance tables that focus on measures of quality based on raw outcomes, i.e. that incorporate the notion of the pupil as a quality-maker. Removing such measures would both counteract the legitimization of associating high-ability intake with high-quality school, and would also reduce the incentive of schools to respond only to the signals from that subset of consumers. This could be supported by adjustments to the funding formula for schools, such that per capita levels are explicitly adjusted across broad pupil types (Le Grand 2007). Second, if the government wants to introduce more options for parents to exercise voice it needs to ensure that the performance management system incorporates incentives for schools to respond to that signal from all consumers (and to respond by improving effectiveness). More generally, it reinforces the importance of considering the design of the top–down elements of reform in conjunction with the bottom–up elements, in order to achieve consistency between user-driven incentives and those created by the performance management system.

Acknowledgements

Thanks to the Leverhulme Trust and ESRC for funding this research through the CMPO. Thanks also for comments on previous drafts to Carol Propper and Helen Simpson. The usual disclaimer applies.

Notes

1. In this chapter I use the terms 'exit' and 'choice' interchangeably, as does most of the literature. I think there are interesting issues regarding whether it is actually exit or entry that is driving choice, but save this for future work (see, however, Teske *et al.* 1993). Also in this chapter I do not emphasize the consequences of considering different types of exit or voice (Dowding and John 2008), nor do I address the 'consumer versus citizen' debate as recently discussed by Greener (2007).
2. The systems are different in each of the countries of the UK; here I focus only on England.
3. The TDA was formed from the merger of the Teacher Training Agency and the National Remodelling Team; more details at www.tda.gov.uk.
4. I shall argue later that the responsiveness of the organization to different signals depends at least partly on the incentives created by the top–down system within which the organization operates (Paul 1992).
5. François (2000, 2001) analyses the effects of individuals placing a value on the quality of service provided even though they do not directly receive personal benefit. His focus is on how such 'care' impacts on employee motivation in the provision of public services.
6. The concepts of quality-maker and quality-taker parallel those of price-maker and price-taker with regard to (im)perfect competition.
7. Many parents, of course, voice their dissatisfaction when they appeal against their child not getting a place at their preferred school, which illustrates one of the

interesting dynamic processes between choice and voice (Dowding *et al.* 2000; Dowding and John 2008).

8. I acknowledge that children are also part of the decision-making process regarding choice of preferred school, but abstract from the issues around the family dynamics of such processes for the purpose of this analysis.

9. Rothstein analyses parental residential location decisions as part of a system of Tiebout choice in the USA.

10. Consumers may not all feel this improvement to the same degree: the evidence suggests that schools exhibit differential effectiveness across the ability distribution, for example (Goldstein and Thomas 1996; Thomas 2001; Wilson and Piebalga 2008).

11. There is a large literature on how public service providers may respond to signals, and targets more generally, in unintended and potentially undesirable ways (see, for example, Smith 1995; Propper and Wilson 2003).

12. Hirschman, for example, discusses the two-party political system in the USA in this context.

13. Propper and Wilson (2003) discuss a similar point regarding general differences between alternative performance measures.

14. See http://news.bbc.co.uk/go/pr/fr/-/1/hi/education/7193052.stm (story published 17 January 2008; accessed 26 June 2008).

15. See http://news.bbc.co.uk/go/pr/fr/-/1/hi/education/7326347.stm (story published 03 April 2008; accessed 26 June 2008).

References

Ball, S. and Vincent, C. (1998), 'I heard it on the grapevine': 'hot' knowledge and school choice, *British Journal of Sociology of Education*, 19, 3: 377–400.

Ball, S., Bowe, R. and Gerwitz, S. (1995), Circuits of schooling: a sociological exploration of parental choice of school in social class contexts, *Sociological Review*, 43: 52–78.

Burgess, S., Briggs, A., McConnell, B. and Slater, H. (2006), *School Choice in England: Background Facts*, CMPO Discussion Paper 06/159, Bristol: CMPO, University of Bristol.

Burgess, S., Propper, C. and Wilson, D. (2007), The impact of school choice in England: the implications from the economic evidence, *Policy Studies*, 28, 2: 129–43.

Butler, T. and Robson, G. (2003), Plotting the middle classes: gentrification and circuits of education in London, *Housing Studies*, 18, 1: 5–28.

Coldron, J. and Boulton, P. (1991), Happiness as a criterion of parental choice of school, *Journal of Education Policy*, 6, 2: 169–78.

Dowding, K. and John, P. (2008), The three exit, three voice and loyalty framework: a test with survey data on local services, *Political Studies*, 56, 2: 288–311.

Dowding, K., John, P., Mergoupis, T. and Vugt, M. van (2000), Exit, voice and loyalty: analytical and empirical developments, *European Journal of Political Research*, 37: 469–95.

François, P. (2000), Public service motivation as an argument for government provision, *Journal of Public Economics*, 78, 3: 275–99.

François, P. (2001), Employee 'care' and the role of non-profit organisations, *Journal of Institutional and Theoretical Economics*, 157: 443–64.

Gaynor, M. (2006), *What Do We Know about Competition and Quality in Health Care Markets?* CMPO Discussion Paper 06/151, Bristol: CMPO, University of Bristol.

Gerwitz, S., Ball, S. and Bowe, R. (1995), *Markets, Choice and Equity in Education*, Buckingham: Open University Press.

Goldstein, H. and Thomas, S. (1996), Using examination results as indicators of school and college performance, *Journal of the Royal Statistical Society*, 159, 1: 149–63.

Greener, I. (2007), Choice and voice – a review, *Social Policy and Society*, 7, 2: 255–65.

Hastings, J. S., Kane, T. J. and Staiger, D. O. (2005), *Parental Preferences and School Competition: Evidence from a Public School Choice Program*, NBER WP 11805, Cambridge, MA: NBER.

Hirschman, A. O. (1970), *Exit, Voice and Loyalty: Responses to Decline in Firms, Organizations and States*, Cambridge, MA: Harvard University Press.

Hotelling, H. (1929), Stability in competition, *Economic Journal*, 39: 41–57.

Hoxby, C. (2003), School choice and school productivity: could school choice be a tide that lifts all boats? In C. Hoxby (ed.), *The Economics of School Choice*, Chicago: University of Chicago Press, pp. 287–342.

Jellison Holme, J. (2002), Buying homes, buying schools: school choice and the social construction of school quality, *Harvard Educational Review*, 72, 2: 177–205.

Le Grand, J. (2007), *The Other Invisible Hand: Delivering Public Services through Choice and Competition*, Princeton, NJ: Princeton University Press.

Paul, S. (1992), Accountability in public services: exit, voice and control, *World Development*, 20, 7: 1047–60.

PMSU (2006), The UK government's approach to public service reform – a discussion paper. Available at: www.strategy.gov.uk/downloads/work_areas/public_service_reform/sj_report.pdf (accessed 15 June 2006).

Propper, C. and Wilson, D. (2003), The use and usefulness of performance measures in the public sector, *Oxford Review of Economic Policy*, 19, 2: 250–67.

Reay, D. and Lucey, H. (2003), The limits of choice: children and inner city schooling, *Sociology*, 37, 1: 121–42.

Rothstein, J. (2004), *Good Principals or Good Peers? Parental Valuation of School Characteristics, Tiebout Equilibrium, and the Effects of Inter-district Competition*, NBER WP 10666, Cambridge, MA: NBER.

Smith, P. (1995), On the unintended consequences of publishing performance data in the public sector, *International Journal of Public Administration*, 18, 2/3: 277–310.

Strategy Unit (2008), *Realising Britain's Potential: Future Strategic Challenges for Britain*, London: Strategy Unit (February).

Teske, P., Schneider, M., Mintrom, M. and Best, S. (1993), Establishing the micro foundations of a macro theory: information, movers, and the competitive local market for public goods, *American Political Science Review*, 87, 3: 702–13.

Thomas, S. (2001), Dimensions of secondary school effectiveness: comparative analyses across regions, *School Effectiveness and School Improvement*, 12: 285–322.

Vincent, C. and Martin, J. (2002), Class, culture and agency: researching parental voice, *Discourse: Studies in the Cultural Politics of Education*, 23, 1: 109–28.

Weekes-Bernard, D. (2007), *School Choice and Ethnic Segregation: Educational Decision-making among Black and Minority Ethnic Parents*, London: Runnymede Trust.

West, A. and Pennell, H. (1999), School admissions: increasing equity, accountability and transparency, *British Journal of Educational Studies*, 46: 188–200.

Wilson, D. and Piebalga, A. (2008), *Accurate Performance Measure but Meaningless Ranking Exercise? An Analysis of the English School League Tables*, CMPO Discussion Paper 07/176, Bristol: CMPO, University of Bristol.

Wilson, D., Croxson, B. and Atkinson, A. (2006), 'What gets measured gets done': headteachers' responses to the English secondary school performance management system, *Policy Studies*, 27, 2: 153–71.

4
When 'Choice' and 'Choice' Are not the Same: Institutional Frameworks of Choice in the German Welfare System

Florian Blank

Introduction

Recent decades have witnessed an increasing use of market mechanisms in the German welfare system. Beginning in the early 1990s and continuing until today, reforms sought to establish new combinations of public and private sectors of welfare provision. These institutional changes often meant creating or strengthening so-called welfare markets, which led to the *de facto* introduction of a considerable amount of choice that 'citizen-consumers' (Clarke 2006) may exercise. This expansion of choice between competing providers and their goods and services took place, even though the notion of choice itself was not high on the German political agenda. Nearly all sectors of the German welfare state were affected by market-enhancing reforms: pension, health-care and long-term care policies as well as employment services. However, in welfare markets 'choice' and 'choice' can mean rather different things for citizens. As will be demonstrated, the choices citizens face are framed by public institutions that give welfare markets in each field of social policy distinctive features. Welfare markets differ regarding the conditions under which citizens engage in market transactions, and which resources they use in them. Acknowledging and investigating these differences in public involvement is of importance since they determine whether the provision of goods and services through welfare markets resembles more a 'traditional' rights-based welfare state or a regular market for consumer goods.

In order to understand the many forms of choice, this chapter analyses the shifts in the German welfare system often subsumed under headings such as 'welfare markets', 'marketization', or 'privatization'. By categorizing the differences between institutional frameworks of choice, it seeks to contribute to a better understanding of the rather different situations which citizens confront in welfare markets. It will be argued that differences between public frameworks can be understood as different values of four parameters: voluntary vs. obligatory exercise of choice; the role of markets relative to public non-market welfare provision; the mode of provision of resources needed to participate in markets; and the mode of calculation of publicly provided resources. This analysis is based on the presentation and comparison of welfare markets in the fields of outpatient health-care services and health insurance schemes, long-term care services, supplementary pension insurance schemes, and employment services. Besides helping to understand the forms marketization takes and its consequences for citizens, this comparison provides hints at the role pre-existing public institutions play in the formation of welfare markets. The cases discussed indicate that welfare markets and respective frameworks of choice are shaped by the characteristics of the institutions of welfare provision existing prior to marketization, even though there is still considerable space for political innovation.

Accordingly, the chapter will be structured as follows. First, an understanding of choice and welfare markets will be introduced that allows for an analysis of frameworks of choice in the German context. This will provide the foundation for the following presentation of welfare markets in health care, long-term care, pension, and employment policies. Programmes will be shown to differ with respect to the four parameters already mentioned. The results of this analysis will be discussed in the final section, which also contains considerations on the influence of pre-existing public institutions of welfare provision on new welfare markets and frameworks of choice.

Choice and Welfare Markets in the German Welfare System

The German system of welfare provision has often been assigned to the conservative or Bismarckian family of welfare states (cf. Esping-Andersen 1990; Palier and Martin 2007). Among its defining characteristics is the major role of public insurance schemes, whose institutional structures as well as contributions and benefits are closely connected to the labour market and employment. However, the branches of the welfare system all display certain individual characteristics, regarding both benefits and institutional features: While insurance schemes aimed at wage replacement such as pension and unemployment insurance schemes link benefits to the individual amount of contributions and are highly centralized, the health sector and the long-term care sector provide benefits on a needs-based basis and are marked by a multitude of public and private insurance companies and service providers. All branches of social insurance have a considerable number of features that do not fit the logic of insurances in a strict sense, such as the inclusion of employees' families in the statutory health insurance scheme, which is not reflected by the individual amount of contributions.

Reforms during the last twenty years did not bring an end to the German welfare system but, even so, had considerable impact on the amount, scope and character of welfare provision (cf. Leibfried and Obinger 2003; Bleses and Seeleib-Kaiser 2004). Besides outright retrenchment and recalibration measures, reforms sought to alter the mixture of public and private elements in welfare provision by introducing market mechanisms in various areas of social policy. Compared to other countries (cf. Taylor-Gooby 1998; 6, 2003; Blomqvist 2004; Clarke 2006; Kremer 2006), the introduction of these market mechanisms was hardly meant to increase citizens' choice. This relative neglect of choice and user empowerment may be explained by two reasons. First, in health care and long-term care services provision, free choice of providers had already been an important feature prior to market-enhancing reforms (health care) or was included in the institutional framework right from its beginning (long-term care). Second, during the most recent decades the costs of the social insurance system and the real or alleged consequences of high non-wage labour costs (i.e. the employers' contributions to the social insurance schemes) for the international competitiveness of the German economy were the dominant theme of social policy discourse. So, generally speaking, choice and user empowerment were by-products of attempts to make welfare provision more efficient and effective, cut costs, lower or stabilize contributions, and improve the quality of services (cf. Kemmerling and Bruttel 2006; Hassenteufel and Palier 2007; Newman and Kuhlmann 2007; Schmähl 2007). For example, in the field of pension policies, 'personal responsibility' (*Eigenverantwortung*) was used instead of 'choice' to characterize the citizen's position and attitude in the post-reform system of welfare provision, lacking some of the positive connotations of 'choice' but stressing the citizen's duties (cf. Nullmeier 2006). Other buzzwords in this field that illustrate the arguments for policy change were 'sustainability' and 'intergenerational equity' (Schmähl 2007). 'Choice' (*Wahlfreiheit*), however, occupied a slightly more prominent place in the context of health-care reforms. Even though in this case the major political reasons for reforms were concerns about efficiency and quality of services (Gerlinger 2009), the introduction of new tariffs in the system of statutory insurance was promoted by referring to the notion of choice (Leiber and Manouguian 2009: 196).

Yet despite the fact that 'choice' did not – and does not – move to the top of the German policy agenda as it did in other countries, today German citizens can frequently exercise choice with respect to welfare. This is a consequence of organizing welfare provision according to economic principles. But while the reorganization of public institutions along the line of New Public Management concepts or an outright privatization may leave the relationship between providers and users unaltered in principle, the establishment of welfare markets affects citizens' access to welfare goods and services. It is these latter welfare markets, places of interaction between competing welfare providers and users, where choice enters the game. This understanding of welfare markets excludes so-called internal markets – sometimes seen as another instance of welfare markets (Nullmeier 2002) since – they do not offer citizens the possibility to exercise choice on their own. Even though there is no shared definition of the concept of choice in social policy research, researchers basically agree in stressing that it refers to situations where users may decide according to their own preferences about alternatives with regard to goods and services and their provision (cf. 6, 2003: 241; Blomqvist 2004: 141).

The terms and quality of the interaction between providers and users, however, must be analysed for every single market in order to draw conclusions on how choice can be exercised by citizens. Nevertheless, there are some conditions welfare markets need to fulfil to qualify as markets and to allow citizens to choose: the supply side must be characterized by competition of providers for consumers, and there must be a direct or indirect exchange of goods and services for resources (cash, vouchers or entitlements). Reference to an indirect exchange and entitlements-*qua*-resources stems from the observation that in some welfare markets access to goods and services is granted as a right, or bills for goods and services are settled by insurance companies. In addition, supply and demand must interact independently; consumers must have at least a certain degree of choice of providers. Competition does not need to be based on prices alone, but also on quality and trust, the latter being especially important if prices are regulated and users can hardly evaluate the quality of products, as often with health services.

These necessary features of markets are complemented by a special form of regulation, which is typical of welfare markets. It is by no means a new phenomenon that markets inevitably succumb to some sort of regulation: 'there is no such thing as an unregulated economy' (Preuss 1985: 163). As the examples will clearly demonstrate, regulation of welfare markets goes beyond regulative policies found in most other markets for goods and services. Welfare markets feature an institutional framework that is characterized by its social policy impetus, but also by regulating both supply *and* demand sides. This kind of public regulation makes welfare markets different from regular consumer markets, where there is often no pronounced demand side intervention. Demand side intervention follows from the social policy objective of providing certain goods and services to citizens in need. A necessary condition for the successful provision of welfare goods and services through markets and for the exercise of choice is assuring citizens' access to markets. This implies a public responsibility for providing the resources necessary to enter into market transactions, this way guaranteeing or allowing a certain level of consumption. The examples discussed below will clearly demonstrate how citizens' market access remains a matter of public responsibility.

Institutional Frameworks of Choice in Germany: Examples

The following examples show the features of welfare markets in the German welfare system. The first one, however, will demonstrate that choice is not really a novelty to the German welfare system, even though there are new possibilities for exercising choice. Discussion will concentrate on health care, health insurance, long-term care, pension, and employment policies, thus dealing with four of the five sectors of social policy covered by the insurance schemes typical of the German welfare state.

Outpatient health-care services

In Germany, outpatient health-care services are basically provided by general practitioners and specialists who run their own practices. This setting was slightly altered by the red–green coalition government in 1999, when hospitals were allowed to offer some special outpatient services (cf. Rosenbrock and Gerlinger 2006: 120–1). Patients are free to a large extent to choose among physicians: they may even decide to consult a specialist directly or get a second opinion from another physician. Access to physicians is granted through participation in a health insurance scheme. Health insurance coverage by a statutory health insurance company has been mandatory for employees up to a certain income and their families; most other citizens (such as civil servants or the self-employed) were covered by private insurance schemes. Insurance coverage was made mandatory for everyone in 2007 (see below). Costs of treatment are settled between physicians and insurance companies in the case of statutory insurance. In the case of private insurance, patients pay for services and get a refund from their insurance company after an assessment of the necessity of the expenses. However, statutory insurance companies have been allowed to offer similar reimbursement tariffs since 2003.

In 2004 free choice among physicians became impeded to a certain degree. Since then, there has been a quarterly flat-rate charge of €10 for statutory insurance patients for outpatient treatment. If a patient chooses to visit another doctor in a quarter they need a referral from the first physician, otherwise they have to pay the fee again. In addition insurance companies experimented with gatekeeper systems that aimed at strengthening the position of family doctors (cf. Newman and Kuhlmann 2007: 13). Nevertheless, there is, all in all, still a fairly high degree of choice in this service market, which became slightly extended through the allowing of hospitals to provide some special outpatient services.

Health insurance

Free choice in health care not only relates to services but also to health insurance contracts, albeit to a smaller degree. The German health insurance system consists of a public sector, basically covering employees and their families, and a private sector, which serves others, such as the self-employed and civil servants. In 2003, statutory and private insurance companies covered nearly the whole population; only 0.2 per cent had no insurance coverage according to Rosenbrock and Gerlinger (2006: 100). Since 2007, insurance coverage has been made mandatory.

Contributions are calculated according to incomes (statutory health insurance; paid for by employees and employers) or risk (private health insurance; employees receive subsidies from their employers towards their contributions). Making insurance coverage mandatory went together with new rules that make sure everyone is able to take out insurance: those who cannot afford contributions are supported by discounts on tariffs or their costs are covered by public institutions. Both public and private insurance companies were also obliged to provide insurance coverage for all citizens belonging to the respective systems.

Since 1970 white-collar workers with an income above a certain threshold may choose to opt out of statutory health insurance and elect to be either privately insured or – until 2007 – to renounce insurance coverage altogether. Since 1989 this possibility has existed for blue-collar employees also. Yet this option was impeded through the health care reform of 2007 by it being made a precondition that a certain income level had to be reached in three consecutive years and would be expected in the following year also.

Within the sector of statutory health insurance, choice has become more important since the 1990s. Until 1992, those who were statutory insured were bound to an insurance company. Since then, as a consequence of an attempt to equalize contributions and to cut costs, they have been able to choose between public insurance companies. The companies differ slightly regarding the amount of contributions and are allowed to offer some special benefits in addition to the basic catalogue of benefits, which continues to account for 95 per cent of expenses (Rosenbrock and Gerlinger 2006: 101). In addition, since 1997 companies have been allowed to offer different contracts to those who are voluntary insured, and later to the statutory insured, among which there are reimbursement and personal share tariffs. The introduction of new contracts may in fact lead to both an increase of choice regarding insurance contracts and a decrease in choice regarding health service provision, because some of the new contracts impede free choice between physicians. Since the creation of competition, the number of public insurance companies has decreased from 1,223 in 1992 to 282 in 2004, due to mergers (Rosenbrock and Gerlinger 2006: 35), thus effectively reducing the scope of choice even though there are still plenty of alternative providers.

Choice in the sector of private insurance is generally impeded, since changing between insurance companies often involves increasing individual contributions. The reason for this can be found in the complex interaction of socio-political regulation and the insurance market mechanisms (cf. Böckmann 2009). However, the 2007 reform brought minor improvements in this sector, too (Leiber and Manouguian 2009: 196).

Long-term care services

In 1995, the social long-term care insurance was introduced. Insurance coverage is connected to health insurance coverage: every member of a statutory health insurance scheme is covered by its long-term care insurance scheme. Those with private insurance coverage have to take out private long-term care insurance. Benefits are differentiated according to three levels of medical condition and to the use of benefits (in-kind benefits have a greater monetary value than cash benefits; benefits for nursing home care are partly higher than benefits for home care). Their calculation does not follow the amount of prior contributions or the actual individual need.

The insured may choose whether to use benefits to buy services from professional care providers that have a contract with the care insurance companies (in-kind benefits), to pass it to relatives or professional care providers without a contract (cash benefits, employer model), or to keep it for themselves – as long as the necessary care services are provided. However, benefits from the long-term care insurance are not meant to cover all expenses that are caused by the need for care. They are seen as a supplement, not least because providing care is still treated as a duty primarily of the family. Additional costs – especially for care in a nursing home – have to be borne by the individual, their family, or social assistance.

The establishment of a care services market was meant to achieve the set-up and provision of an efficient care infrastructure. This infrastructure should be marked by competition, efficiency and capability, besides quality and humanity, according to the justification of the draft bill for the establishment of the long-term care insurance (Deutscher Bundestag 1993: 3, cf. 136). The introduction of the social long-term care insurance led to a sharp increase in the number of care providers. However, according to Rothgang and Igl (2007: 59), the doubling of the respective figures in the immediate aftermath of the introduction of the long-term care insurance may be due to the reorganization of already-existing care providers such as informal care systems run by the churches. For 1999–2005, they report a slightly growing number of providers of home care, with an increase in employees of 16.6 per cent and a decrease in full-time employees of 1.0 per cent. The number of providers of nursing home care, however, rose by 17.7 per cent and the number of beds by 17.3 per cent in this period (2007: 60).

Supplementary pension insurance

The 2001 pension reform of the red–green coalition government has been dubbed by some observers a paradigm shift (Schmähl 2004, 2007). Here, the existing pay-as-you-go statutory scheme covering basically all blue and white-collar workers was altered in a way that will probably lead to lower future benefits. To help citizens to compensate for declining benefits, a governmentally fostered, privately funded pension scheme was introduced, called *Riester-Rente* after the then Minister of Work and Social Affairs, Walter Riester. Citizens may (or may not) decide to invest their financial resources in insurance schemes offered by commercial insurance companies. If they decide to do so, they receive governmental subsidies or tax-breaks. These benefits are designed in a way that favours families with low incomes and children. In order to be fostered, insurance contracts have to be designed according to governmental regulations. Among these are the rules that the insurance company has to guarantee that a pension will be paid from the end of one's working life until death, and that when reaching pensionable age, at least the sum contributed (plus governmental subsidies) is available. Contracts must be certified by a special governmental agency, the Federal Financial Supervisory Authority. This promotion of investments does not apply for the whole population; it is aimed especially at members of the statutory pension scheme and their spouses, civil servants, but also people providing care-work in their family or raising children up to the age of three. According to a press release of the Ministry of Work and Social Affairs, up to autumn 2008, some 12 million governmentally fostered insurance contracts were concluded (BMAS 2008).

Employment services

Since the 1990s, employment services have been subject to various reforms that brought an end to the former public monopoly in this field (Kaps and

Schütz 2007: 5). These reforms permitted the establishment of commercial employment agencies and later deregulated this trade. A 2001 law gave the unemployed the right to demand the involvement of commercial employment agencies after six months of unemployment. Since 2002 unemployed people who receive benefits from the unemployment insurance have a right to vouchers for the use of the services of commercial employment agencies after three months of unemployment. The waiting period was later cut and amounts to two months at the moment. People who receive the means-tested basic income for job-seekers (*Arbeitslosengeld II*) may also be given these vouchers; however, they do not have a right to them. Today, these vouchers have a value of €2,000. If used, the commercial employment agency receives half of this amount after the unemployed person has been in a new job for six weeks, the other half after six months of employment.

For the period between 2002 and 2004 – when the design of vouchers was slightly different than today – Kaps and Schütz (2007: 21) report that vouchers were handed to 1.4 million unemployed persons. Of these vouchers, 8 per cent were used, of which 43 per cent led to an employment lasting longer than six months.

Differences between Frameworks of Choice

The examples all fit the given overall understanding of welfare markets: citizen-consumers buy goods and services from competing suppliers, their exercise of choice being supported in one way or another by a framework of public institutions. However, even this short overview reveals important differences in the design of the institutional frameworks. They differ with respect to the following four parameters. First, market access and thus exercise of choice is voluntary in some cases and obligatory in others. Second, welfare markets play different roles relative to public non-market provision of welfare. Third, welfare markets differ regarding the mode of provision of resources needed to engage in market transactions. Finally, the publicly provided resources are calculated in different ways. The different values of these parameters have important consequences for the exercise of choice and in general for the access to goods and services. They help to understand whether concrete instances of choice constitute a new form of what basically remains publicly provided welfare, or mean a privatization of risks.

Voluntary vs. obligatory exercise of choice

The most obvious difference between the markets presented is whether citizens exercise choice voluntarily or as an obligation. Voluntary exercise of choice can be found in four of the five markets discussed. With respect to health and long-term care services, individuals principally make their own decisions as to whether and how to use the entitlements or, rather, the insurance benefits in the care service markets. In the case of the *Riester-Rente*, the decision to enter the market is voluntary, too, but under the condition that citizens invest their own money. The vouchers for employment services for recipients of unemployment insurance benefits resemble these programmes insofar as the decision to enter the welfare market or to continue to rely on public employment services is also left to the individual.

Making insurance coverage obligatory for all in the sector of health insurance, on the one hand, made participation in the insurance market and thus choice among insurance companies and contracts obligatory for all citizens. On the other hand, it reduced choice for a small part of the population who could until then decide not to take out insurance. Mandatory health insurance for all is made possible by providing the resources for contributions on a needs-based basis in some cases. Compulsory insurance was also an option discussed in the run-up to the introduction of the *Riester-Rente* (Nullmeier 2002: 275).

The difference between compulsory and voluntary exercise of choice is of importance especially in insurance markets because it touches on the question of what constitutes a social risk. Here, public responsibility for citizens' security may be realized through compulsory market activity, which serves as an equivalent to a 'traditional' social right.

The role of markets: markets as alternatives, supplements or sole solutions

The need to exercise choice may follow not only from officially obligating citizens to participate in markets. It may also be a consequence of the role welfare markets play relative to public non-market institutions of welfare provision. Here, we find three values: First, there are markets that make up the complete provision of services, as in the case of health and long-term care service and insurance markets. So even if insurance coverage had not been made mandatory, the exercise of choice in the health insurance market would be a necessity to many because no provision of insurance coverage is given outside the market. Second, the market for private pension insurance contracts was meant to supplement the further existing statutory pension insurance – entering this market is not a matter of all-or-nothing since a public institution continues to provide benefits. Finally, in the case of employment services, recipients of unemployment insurance benefits have a 'choice to choose': they have a right to vouchers to be used in a service market but may decide to rely on public services, so here the market constitutes an alternative.

This distinction of different roles of welfare markets is important insofar as it directly affects citizens' confrontation with choice. Thus it also affects the need to consider public involvement in providing the material resources to enter markets.

Modes of provision of resources

Besides an obligation or need to enter markets, citizens' market activities are influenced by the public provision of resources to be used in welfare markets. The above examples show that there are differences regarding the provision of resources. Resources needed for market access may be completely or partly provided by public institutions – this may be seen as a quasi-public demand that becomes effective through the individual's market activities. In contrast, in other markets, market access is primarily based on resources that stem from the individual's income or other private sources, and public benefits serve merely as an upgrade of investments. Here we can speak of publicly supported private demand.

In the case of health-care services, market access is basically a matter of entitlements obtained through membership of an insurance scheme. Since insurance coverage could factually be seen as being granted for the great majority of the population and was finally made mandatory in 2007, this closely resembles a social right to services realized through general insurance coverage. (This basically applies to the long-term care insurance, too.) However, since the introduction of the practice charge, citizens also have to invest their own resources to access services. In the statutory health insurance scheme, the combination of obligatory insurance membership for employees, co-financing by employees and employers, the inclusion of family members, as well as public coverage of contributions for the unemployed serves as a functional equivalent to the provision of public resources to be used in the insurance market.

Choice is basically the consequence of a social right also in the case of vouchers for employment services. Beneficiaries of the unemployment insurance have, after a period of unemployment, a right to a voucher to be used to pay commercial employment agencies. Public provision of resources is designed differently where vouchers are allocated to recipients of basic income for job-seekers: here the exercise of choice depends on the decision of the public employment agency's staff.

The example of the *Riester-Rente*, finally, demonstrates the second value of this parameter: governmental subsidies can be seen as a reward for the individual decision to get active in markets and invest private resources that could be used in other ways.

These observations indicate that a traditional social rights-based approach to welfare provision may be compatible with welfare markets and choice. In this case, social rights are not claims to goods and services directed against public institutions, but rights to market access, which is guaranteed by public institutions.

Calculation of publicly provided resources

Finally, the exercise of choice depends not least on the amount of resources given to market participants. Resources can have a monetary value or they can consist of entitlements to needs-based service delivery. In the cases of long-term care insurance and vouchers for employment services, resources are provided at a flat rate, even though benefits of the long-term care insurance are differentiated. However, while benefits from the long-term care insurance were explicitly meant to provide only part of the resources needed in the market for care services, in employment services the cost of services acquired with the vouchers may not exceed the value of the voucher. So even if resources are given as a social right, this does not mean that the exercise of choice through the use of these resources might lead to a full satisfaction of the citizens' needs. This problem does not arise where entitlements are the basis for market activities and guarantee direct access to service provision. This is the case with the statutory health insurance that entitles citizens to access outpatient health services.

Finally, the amount of subsidies and tax-breaks in the case of the *Riester-Rente* depends on the individual income and investments. Families with children enjoy additional benefits.

Discussion: The Diverse Institutional Frameworks of Choice

The examples demonstrate quite clearly that choice is in fact an important feature of welfare provision in Germany, but also that there are important differences between the public frameworks of welfare markets where citizens exercise choice. These differences can be categorized using four parameters depicting different aspects of public involvement. Table 1 summarizes the most important results.

The evidence given shows that the design of public institutional frameworks plays a major role in shaping the conditions under which citizens exercise choice and is thus responsible for the ensuing challenges for citizen-consumers – the examples show clearly that 'choice' and 'choice' are not the same. The values of the parameters show that there are quite different answers to the question of who enters into market transactions under which conditions. Some institutional arrangements seem to be more akin to traditional social policy than others, thus potentially connecting the advantages of choice with the security associated with the welfare state. For example, a combination of a market, where public insurance companies compete, and mandatory insurance and public support for citizens who cannot afford contributions may fit the traditional understanding of public responsibility for individual welfare (cf. Taylor-Gooby 1999: 111) as in the case of statutory health insurance. In contrast, if the decision to enter a market for insurance contracts offered by commercial companies is left to the citizens who also have to invest their private resources, such a setting displays similarities to a regular market for insurance contracts despite socio-political regulation of this market, as in the case of supplementary pension insurance.

It should be clear that this analysis of the institutional settings of choice does not answer important questions on the individual cognitive and material preconditions to deal successfully with the offers of competing suppliers of welfare goods and services. The problems possibly or actually arising from a mismatch between citizens' expectations and abilities on the one hand, and policy-makers' beliefs about the latter on the other, have often been discussed in analyses of new welfare markets, not least because they point towards essential normative questions about equity and justice in welfare provision (Klein and Millar 1995; Taylor-Gooby 1999, 2001; Hinrichs 2004). An analysis of the institutional frameworks of choice also omits the features of the goods and services subject to choice: while in insurance markets highly standardized products without a limit to production may lead to little or no competition among consumers, care service markets may pose the problem that a given supplier is only able to deal with a certain number of clients. This may prompt the consequence that citizens compete with each other for the best provider,

Table 1

Summary: differences between frameworks of choice in the German welfare system

	Voluntary vs. obligatory exercise of choice	Role of markets	Mode of provision of resources used in market transactions	Calculation of publicly provided resources to be used in markets
Outpatient health care services	• voluntary exercise	• no service provision outside service market	• entitlement follows from compulsory insurance membership • *but* practice charge	• direct entitlements to needs-based service delivery
Health insurance	• obligatory exercise	• no provision of insurance contracts outside public and private insurance markets • little choice between public and private markets	• statutory health insurance: compulsory insurance coverage for employees and their families financed by employees and employers • private health insurance: investment of private resources, subsidies of employers • entitlement to needs-based support in case of lack of resources	• [compulsory insurance serves as functional equivalent for public provision of resources] • needs-based support and special tariffs in case of lack of resources and unemployment
Long-term care services	• voluntary exercise	• service provision outside service market by the family is possible	• resources (cash or entitlements to in-kind services) follow from compulsory insurance membership • *but* factual need to invest private resources in many cases	• flat-rate benefits differentiated according to levels of medical condition and usage of benefits
Supplementary pension insurance	• voluntary exercise	• insurance market is a supplement to the public insurance scheme	• entitlement to tax breaks and subsidies as 'gratification' for the investment of private resources	• amount of tax breaks and subsidies depends on amount of investments and family size
Employment services	• voluntary exercise	• service market is an alternative to service provision by public agencies	• entitlement to resources (receivers of benefits from the unemployment insurance) • expert's decision about resources (receivers of basic income for job-seekers)	• flat-rate voucher

which means some may enjoy goods and services of a better quality than others – this is part of the definition of competition. That this is not only a theoretical problem is demonstrated by the various measures that exist to control the quality of goods and services, from the governmental certification of insurance contracts to requirements for care service providers regarding their internal quality management. Characteristics of the goods may affect choice in a second way, too: services that are to be consumed directly, sometimes in emergency situations, will challenge the citizens' ability to make reasonable decisions differently than choices that are related to future risks.

I want to concentrate in the last paragraphs on taking an exploratory look at whether there are any explanations for differences between instances of public frameworks of choice in Germany. The examples presented point towards a strong influence of already existing institutions on new welfare markets and frameworks of choice, which nevertheless leaves room for a considerable degree of political innovation. The different values of the parameter 'role of markets' provide a first hint that pre-existing welfare institutions shape welfare markets and the conditions of choice – where a multitude of different public or non-profit providers already existed, as in the case of health and long-term care services and insurance systems, choice was enhanced by creating competition between these providers and by allowing new providers to join the competition. Regarding the supplementary pension insurance and vouchers for private employment agencies, markets were established as addendums to public monopoly providers (or in the case of pensions: oligopoly) that continue to deliver benefits and services. So markets were created outside the existing systems.

Looking more closely at the public institutional frameworks, the institutional frameworks of choice in health-care services and insurance markets still show many features of the settings prior to the market-enhancing reforms since the 1990s, which may be due to marketization having taken place within the respective systems. In contrast, the 1995 introduction of the social long-term care scheme meant establishing a new public framework. Even though this framework was designed after the example of the health-care system, the new set-up made political innovation possible, especially regarding the desired role of the family in service provision. As a consequence, the resources for market activities are not given as direct entitlements (as in the statutory health insurance schemes) but as subsidies with a fixed monetary value.

Public institutional frameworks of choice in pension and employment policies, where new markets were created, are also related to the pre-existing and persisting public institutions. In the case of the *Riester-Rente*, public subsidies for private investments are available basically for members of the mandatory pension scheme and some other groups, but not for the whole population. And vouchers for employment services are given to those who qualify for services delivered by the public employment agencies. The difference between these two frameworks regarding the public provision of resources can be explained by looking at the reasons for marketization in these fields: while in the case of supplementary pension insurance, cutting public expenses stood in the foreground and therefore individual investment was to be encouraged, the rationale behind introducing a voucher scheme in employment services was to create a more efficient system of service delivery and activate the unemployed.

So according to this account, the pre-existing (public) settings of welfare provision shape welfare markets and the respective public frameworks (cf. Köppe 2008). Nevertheless, political decisions are responsible especially for the kind and amount of resources provided in new markets. The complex interlocking of older public institutions with new markets and the public frameworks of choice show that in Germany marketization goes together with continuing public involvement in questions of social security. Even though there may be new ways of welfare provision, citizens' social protection and their relation to providers of welfare goods and services remain subject to social policy. Since there is a huge variety of possibilities to design frameworks of choice and to realize public responsibility in the context of new markets, social policy analysis is well advised to examine every new instance of marketization and choice to understand the challenges citizens face.

References

Bleses, P. and Seeleib-Kaiser, M. (2004), *The Dual Transformation of the German Welfare State*, Basingstoke: Palgrave Macmillan.

Blomqvist, P. (2004), The choice revolution: privatization of Swedish welfare services in the 1990s, *Social Policy & Administration*, 38, 2: 139–55.

Böckmann, R. (2009), Die Private Krankenversicherung – weder Solidarität noch Wettbewerb [Private health insurance – neither solidarity nor competition]. In R. Böckmann (ed.), *Gesundheitsversorgung zwischen Solidarität und Wettbewerb* [Health care between solidarity and competition], Wiesbaden: VS, pp. 63–90.

Bundesministerium für Arbeit und Soziales [BMAS, Federal Ministry of Work and Social Affairs] (2008), Weiter großer Zuspruch: knapp 12 Millionen Riester-Renten! [Huge popularity continues: almost 12 million *Riester-Renten!*] Press release, 12 November. Available at: www.bmas.de/coremedia/generator/29428/2008_11_12_riesterzahlen.html (accessed 30 January 2009).

Clarke, J. (2006), Consumers, clients or citizens? Politics, policy and practice in the reform of social care, *European Societies*, 8, 3: 423–42.

Deutscher Bundestag (1993), *Gesetzentwurf der Fraktionen der CDU/CDU und FDP, Entwurf eines Gesetzes zur sozialen Absicherung des Risikos der Pflegebedürftigkeit (Pflege-Versicherungsgesetz – PflegeVG)* [Draft bill of the parliamentary groups of the CDU/CSU and FDP, Draft of a law for social protection against the risk of need of care (Long-Term Care Insurance Law)], Drucksache 12/5262, Bonn.

Esping-Andersen, G. (1990), *The Three Worlds of Welfare Capitalism*, Cambridge: Polity Press.

Gerlinger, T. (2009), Wettbewerb und Patientenorientierung in der gesetzlichen Krankenversicherung [Competition and patient orientation in the statutory health insurance]. In R. Böckmann (ed.), *Gesundheitsversorgung zwischen Solidarität und Wettbewerb* [Health care between solidarity and competition], Wiesbaden: VS, pp. 19–41.

Hassenteufel, P. and Palier, B. (2007), Towards Neo-Bismarckian health care states? Comparing health insurance reforms in Bismarckian welfare systems, *Social Policy & Administration*, 41, 6: 574–96.

Hinrichs, K. (2004), *Active Citizens and Retirement Planning: Enlarging Freedom of Choice in the Course of Pension Reforms in Nordic Countries and Germany*, ZeS-Working Paper, 11/2004, Bremen: Universität Bremen/Zentrum für Sozialpolitik.

Kaps, P. and Schütz, H. (2007), *Privatisierung von Arbeitsvermittlungsdienstleistungen – Wundermittel zur Effizienzsteigerung? Eine Bestandsaufnahme deutscher und internationaler Erfahrungen* [Privatization of employment services – panacea to improve efficiency? A review of German and international experiences], Wissenschaftszentrum Berlin für Sozialforschung (WZB)/Forschungsschwerpunkt Arbeit, Sozialstruktur und Sozialstaat, Abteilung Arbeitsmarktpolitik und Beschäftigung: Discussion paper, Berlin.

Kemmerling, A. and Bruttel, O. (2006), 'New politics' in German labour market policy? The implications of the recent Hartz reforms for the German welfare state, *West European Politics*, 29, 1: 90–112.

Klein, R. and Millar, J. (1995), Do-it-yourself policy: searching for a new paradigm? *Social Policy & Administration*, 29, 4: 303–16.

Köppe, S. (2008), New phenomena and old theories: welfare markets and welfare state change. Paper given at the 2nd ECPR Graduate Conference, Barcelona, 25–27 August.

Kremer, M. (2006), Consumers in charge of care: the Dutch personal budget and its impact on the market, professionals and the family, *European Societies*, 8, 3: 385–401.

Leiber, M. and Manouguian, M.-S. (2009), Vereinbarkeit von Wettbewerb und Solidarität in der sozialen Krankenversicherung? Gesundheitsreformen in den Niederlanden und Deutschland [Compatibility of competition and solidarity in the social health insurance system? Health-care reforms in the Netherlands and Germany]. In R. Böckmann (ed.), *Gesundheitsversorgung zwischen Solidarität und Wettbewerb* [Health care between solidarity and competition], Wiesbaden: VS, pp. 175–202.

Leibfried, S. and Obinger, H. (2003), The state of the welfare state: German social policy between macroeconomic retrenchment and microeconomic recalibration, *West European Politics*, 26, 4: 199–218.

Newman, J. and Kuhlmann, E. (2007), Consumers enter the political stage? The modernization of health care in Britain and Germany, *Journal of European Social Policy*, 17, 2: 99–111.

Nullmeier, F. (2002), Auf dem Weg zu Wohlfahrtsmärkten? [On the way to health-care markets?]. In W. Süß (ed.), *Deutschland in den neunziger Jahren* [Germany in the 1990s], Opladen: Leske + Budrich, pp. 269–81.

Nullmeier, F. (2006), Personal responsibility and its contradiction in terms, *German Policy Studies/Politikfeldanalyse*, 3, 3: 386–99.

Palier, B. and Martin, C. (2007), From 'a frozen landscape' to structural reform: the sequential transformation of Bismarckian welfare systems, *Social Policy & Administration*, 41, 6: 535–54.

Preuss, U. K. (1985), The concept of rights and the welfare state. In G. Teubner (ed.), *Dilemmas of Law in the Welfare State*, Berlin and New York: Walter de Gruyter, pp. 151–72.

Rosenbrock, R. and Gerlinger, T. (2006), *Gesundheitspolitik, Eine systematische Einführung* [Health policy, a systematic introduction], Bern: Hans Huber.

Rothgang, H. and Igl, G. (2007), Long-term care in Germany, *Japanese Journal of Social Security Policy*, 6, 1: 54–84.

Schmähl, W. (2004), Paradigm shift in German pension policy: measures aiming at a new public–private mix and their effects. In M. Rein and W. Schmähl (eds), *Rethinking the Welfare State, The Political Economy of Pension Reform*, Cheltenham: Edward Elgar, pp. 153–204.

Schmähl, W. (2007), Dismantling an earnings-related social pension scheme: Germany's new pension policy, *Journal of Social Policy*, 36, 2: 319–40.

6, Perri (2003), Giving consumers of British public services more choice: what can be learned from recent history? *Journal of Social Policy*, 32, 2: 239–70.

Taylor-Gooby, P. (1998), Choice and the policy agenda. In P. Taylor-Gooby (ed.), *Choice and Public Policy: The Limits to Welfare Markets*, Basingstoke: Macmillan, pp. 1–23.

Taylor-Gooby, P. (1999), Markets and motives, trust and egoism in welfare markets, *Journal of Social Policy*, 28, 1: 97–114.

Taylor-Gooby, P. (2001), Risk, contingency and the Third Way: evidence from the BHPS and qualitative studies, *Social Policy & Administration*, 35, 2: 195–211.

5
Choosing Welfare or Losing Social Citizenship? Citizens' Free Choice in Recent Italian Welfare State Reforms

Paolo R. Graziano

The Italian Welfare State and Citizens' Free Choice: An Introduction

Just as in many other continental and southern European welfare states (Esping-Andersen 1990; Ferrera 1996), the Italian welfare state has traditionally been one in which citizens' interests were strongly mediated by well-established interest groups – trade unions and other crucial political actors such as political parties (Ferrera 1984; Ascoli 1985). This decision-making configuration left very little room for manoeuvre for non-unionized and non-politicized citizens: in a nutshell, they had to accept what was formulated and implemented by national and local decision-makers. The lack of freedom in articulating political preferences concerned both welfare state recipients and welfare state services and/or benefits providers. It could be argued that some 'freedom of choice' was left in the implementation phase but it was not the case in any of the selected policy areas until the mid-1990s: with respect to employment protection, all benefits and services were implemented by national (or sub-national) public authorities whereas private employment services were outlawed (Gualmini 1998); the basic pension system was public and the pension schemes were not very flexible (Jessoula 2009); health-care policies were fully managed by public actors and private health-care expenditure has historically been very limited (Maino 2001; OECD 2008). Therefore, at first sight, the traditional Italian welfare state left very little space for citizens to exercise freedom of choice, the overall system being basically publicly managed and leaving citizens (or welfare state recipients) with a highly standardized social policy menu. Furthermore, private welfare state service providers were also quite marginal since the overall management of social policy schemes was guaranteed by the public administration.

To be sure, these Italian features are by no means surprising. If we look at the (limited) literature on welfare state developments and its links with freedom of choice we learn that the only welfare state regime or model which left more space for citizens' or recipients' free choice is the liberal or Anglo-Saxon one[1] in which the protection of social rights was grounded in an ideological context placing freedom – and therefore free choice – at the heart of the political system (Marshall 1950). Only more recently, due to the reforms of the 1990s, in other welfare state models or regimes freedom of choice – conceived basically as privatization and multiplication of social policy options – has been expanded (Blomqvist 2004; Thompson and Mossialos 2006; Morel 2007; Greener and Powell 2008).

Nevertheless, the 1990s have been quite interesting with respect to welfare reforms in Italy. With the partial exception of national social assistance (Ferrera 2005), numerous aspects of Italian social policies have been significantly changed. But the underlying push for reform, as we will illustrate in greater detail in the following sections, was not 'freedom of choice' but 'modernization' or cost containment since the overall public expenditure was very high and out of line with other European countries and, even specifically, with the Maastricht criteria (Ferrera and Gualmini 2004; Rossi 2007). Therefore, due to the peculiarity of the Italian case, the main goal of any welfare state reform was to recalibrate the system without increasing the overall public expenditure on welfare policies (Ferrera 1998; Boeri 2000; Ferrera and Hemerijck 2003).

There were, however, political opportunities for further changes in the underlying principles of social protection: the political scandals of the early 1990s – which delegitimized the traditional ruling parties (such as the *Democrazia Cristiana*, the Christian Democratic Party) – and the creation of new leading political parties (such as *Forza Italia*), created unprecedentedly favourable conditions for the construction of a pro-freedom of choice political discourse[2] and policy proposals. More specifically, between 1992 and 1994, the Italian political system was shaken by a 'political earthquake' connected to the corruption scandals which affected many important ruling Italian political parties (Cotta and Isernia 1996; Cotta and Verzichelli 2007). Among other consequences, one of the main effects of the above-mentioned phenomenon was that old (ruling and non-ruling) parties either changed their name or disappeared and new parties entered on to the scene. The most important party was *Forza Italia*, which just before the 1994 elections created a electoral coalition named *Polo delle Libertà* (Pole of Liberty) which obtained a strong parliamentary majority. Furthermore, another party supporting the *Polo delle Libertà* (*Lega Nord* – Northern League) was tirelessly denouncing the excessive costs of 'Rome' (i.e. the political and administrative system, based in Rome) asking for more territorial freedom and autonomy over several public policies, including social protection. In fact, since 1994 the Italian political discourse has often been centred on the concept of freedom of choice. For example, the leader of *Forza Italia*, Silvio Berlusconi, gave a famous speech in that year communicating to the Italian population that he was going to enter into politics principally in order to avoid an 'illiberal' Italy.[3] From then on, liberty and freedom of choice gained new legitimacy in the Italian political arena.

More generally, if we look at the various elections held from 1994 to 2008, we do see how neo-liberal discourse became much more relevant over the years (Segatti 1995; Legnante and Sani 2002), although it has lost some of its innovative traits more recently (Legnante and Sani 2007). What is particularly striking is the convergence among the various political actors (with the exception of the extreme left party *Rifondazione Comunista*) on the need for more liberty for Italian citizens over the course of their lives. For example, in the most recent national electoral campaign (2008), Walter Veltroni – the leader of the *Partito Democratico* (pivotal actor of the centre-left Coalition) – clearly stated that one of the main problems of Italy is 'the limited citizen's freedom of designing his/her own life'.[4] Therefore, since the early 1990s the Italian political landscape has increasingly pointed to the need for more citizens' and territorial freedom, and such need has been shared by all the most important Italian parties, such as *Popolo delle Libertà*, *Partito Democratico* (or the former parties which set up the *Partito Democratico* in 2008) and the *Lega Nord*. But how consistent is this new political discourse with respect to the welfare state reforms formulated, adopted and implemented in Italy over the past fifteen years? How have these generic claims in favour of freedom been translated into 'new' social protection policies? And has freedom of choice been translated into coherent policy reforms? In order to answer this question we need to take a closer look at the development of the various social policies which lie at the heart of any welfare state configuration: employment, pensions and health care.

Freedom of Choice and Social Policies

Before analysing the most important welfare reforms in the above-mentioned policy fields, we need to clarify our definition of freedom of choice. At least two dimensions have to be considered, especially with respect to the Italian case: welfare state services and benefits supply. First, citizens can be provided with a greater or lesser freedom of choice with respect to the welfare state by having various choice options, due to the presence of different service providers. For example, in the employment policy field, citizens can choose among various providers of vocational training courses or public employment services whose costs are fully (or partially) covered by the public authorities – either at the local or at the national level. In health-care policies, citizens may be able to choose among various health-care service providers (such as doctors, hospitals, etc.). To be sure, in other countries the freedom of choice rhetoric has been used primarily in sectors such as education, care services, health care and housing, in particular in the Anglo-Saxon welfare state model (Greener and Powell 2008), although more recently also more 'Bismarckian' (Thompson and Mossialos 2006; Morel 2007) and Scandinavian countries (Blomqvist 2004) have significantly made arguments in favour of an increased degree of citizens' choice in welfare state services. Second, citizens can also have different degrees of freedom with respect to the choice of benefit providers: the most appropriate example is in pensions policy, where with respect to the second (and third) pillar, citizens might decide which retirement schemes and investment funds are the most appropriate for their personal purposes; in other terms, in the field of pensions, citizens may have an option to select their preferred pension scheme from various insurance companies – the extreme case being an almost entirely private pension system, as in the

United States. This implies that citizens' freedom of choice is also linked to the presence of a plurality of providers among which each citizen can choose his or her most preferred services and benefits. As mentioned above, the (limited) empirical literature on the freedom of choice debate focuses mainly on the first dimension (i.e. welfare state services supply: see Thomson and Mossialos 2006; Morel 2007; Greener and Powell 2008), whereas the second dimension (welfare state benefits supply) has not been particularly present in the debate on pensions policy – centred more on the equity, sustainability and management of reforms than on the capacity of reforms to insure greater or lesser freedom of choice for citizens (Immergut *et al.* 2006).

In the analysis of the Italian case, employment, pensions and health care have been selected among other policies for three main reasons. First, they still are the most relevant national welfare state policies, even in those cases where decentralization processes have occurred – such as in employment services or health-care policy. Second, they are the policies which have been significantly involved in reform processes over the past fifteen years and therefore it seems particularly interesting to see if and how the 'freedom of choice' rhetoric was translated into 'new' social policies. Third, the above-mentioned policies have been the most controversial, since societal and political interests differed greatly and various arguments, among which we may find the 'freedom of choice' one, have been made in order to support and defend political actors' preferences.

Before diving into the policy details, we must clearly distinguish the 'freedom of choice' rhetoric from the real opportunity for citizens to be free to make decisions concerning welfare state services or benefits. In this chapter, we will primarily analyse the presence/absence of a freedom of choice rhetoric or political discourse since it would be very difficult to assess its implementation without appropriate methodological tools (survey data and/or individual preference data). Nevertheless, Eurobarometer survey data will be used as a proxy of workers' preferences, and explicit reference to the implementation of some policies which have increased the degree of freedom of choice for Italian citizens will be made (for example, in the case of pensions). However, we will not be systematic in this exercise throughout the chapter due to a lack of comparative data for all the examined policies.

Finally, the sources used for this chapter are primarily policy documents (i.e. legislative texts, governmental policy briefs and documents supporting policy proposals) and secondary sources (i.e. contributions to the Italian welfare state literature which have illustrated, commented and/or explained the recent Italian reform processes).

Employment Policy and Freedom of Choice

The 1990s have been years of important changes in Italian employment protection policy. In very general terms, there is a broad consensus in the literature on the new trend of Italian employment policy regulation towards more flexibility for 'outsiders' or 'newcomers' (i.e. those who are unemployed or are being employed for the first time), maintaining security for 'older' workers and increasing unemployment benefits for the 'standard'[5] workers (Ferrera

Table 1

Incidence of 'atypical', flexible contracts

	1993	1998	2003	2006
Permanent, part-time	3.2	4.7	6.3	7.9
Temporary	6.1	8.6	9.9	9.5
Total	9.3	13.3	16.2	17.4

Note: Temporary contracts refer to: fixed-term employees and atypical (*contratto di collaborazione a progetto*) workers.
Source: Graziano *et al.* (2008: 9).

and Gualmini 2004; Graziano 2007; Samek Lodovici and Semenza 2008). More specifically, two important reforms have taken place over the past 15 years: the Law 196/1997 and the Law 30/2003. The first Law (196/1997), formulated and approved under a centre-left government, was primarily aimed at deregulating Italian employment policy by increasing flexibility options thanks to the reduction of overall strictness of regulation on temporary employment and to the introduction of temporary work agencies which were outlawed before the approval of the reform. The second Law (30/2003), formulated and approved by a centre-right government, introduced even more flexibility by multiplying the employment contract options and therefore providing more 'freedom of choice' with respect to conditions of employment contracts.[6] To be sure, more freedom of choice was provided to employers than to employees since the negotiating power of both unionized and non-unionized workers has not been particularly strong in the past decade (Mania and Sateriale 2002). Nevertheless, at least some citizens (i.e. employers) had more freedom of choice with respect to the available contract options.

The overall effect of these reforms is an increase in the incidence of 'precarious', flexible contracts (see table 1), the reduction of the overall strictness of regulation on temporary employment and no change in the overall strictness of regulation on collective dismissals (figure 1).

But how are these reforms connected to the underlying political discourse or arguments used by key decision-makers during the policy formulation and adoption phase? In fact, if we focus on the two major reforms, the key argument was 'modernization' of the Italian employment protection system. In the words of the former Labour Minister: '[the Law 196/1997] is mainly aimed at increasing job opportunities and it does so by adopting different instruments' (Treu 2001: 26). Also in the governmental White Book on the Labour Market in Italy (Ministero del Welfare 2001) the 'modernization' aim is at the core of the arguments expressed in favour of a further reform which will take place in 2003: 'The Italian labour market requires … important changes in its legislative framework by moving systematically towards a modernization of work organization and employment relationships' (Ministero del Welfare 2001: xii).

Figure 1

Employment protection legislation index, Italy, 1990–2003

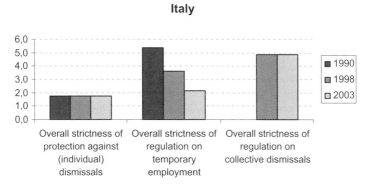

Source: Graziano *et al.* (2008: 9).

Furthermore, the modernization argument is also strongly connected to the need for Italy to become much more similar to other European countries and follow the European Employment Strategy prescriptions aimed at the promotion of activation policies: 'The general approach of the centre-left governments [1996–2001] responds to … indications coming from European directives' (Treu 2001: 25); 'moving from European guidelines, the government intends to proceed … towards a legislature programme aimed at the promotion of an active society where there are more job opportunities for all, a better overall job quality is offered and more modern rules which regulate the organization of employment relationships and labour markets are implemented' (Ministero del Welfare 2001: v).

In other words, the main arguments in favour of the most important labour market reforms of the past decade are connected to the need to make Italy more 'modern' and place it in line with European standards. No (implicit or explicit) reference is made to workers' preferences, taking for granted that the goals will be shared by all the political and social actors involved. And, indeed, they might have been shared – also by the precarious workers – if in connection to the flexibilization of the Italian labour market more had been done on the security dimension, unlike what actually happened in Italy (Samek Lodovici and Semenza 2008; Graziano *et al.* 2008).

To be sure, the legalization of temporary work agencies and the (partial) privatization of employment services (Pirrone and Sestito 2006) could be seen as an opportunity to increase job opportunities and perhaps enhance freedom of choice among job seekers since they could profit from the increase in job offers. But again the main impetus for these decisions was not to increase choice opportunities but rather to increase job opportunities – whatever the personal preference of the job-seeker was. Therefore, the main beneficiaries in terms of freedom of choice have been the employers, not the workers.

Furthermore, the decentralization of vocational training services has provided an opportunity to increase the freedom of choice of job-seekers in selecting professional training (at least in some regions, for example Lombardy; see Colombo 2008), but such freedom was only connected to the choice of vocational training areas and services rather than concrete job opportunities. Finally, if we look more at the details of the preferences of the Italian population, according to recent Eurobarometer data we find out that in 2008 unemployment was still considered to be a chief concern (after those of inflation and the overall economic situation; European Commission 2008: 29) and the overall perception among Italian citizens – half of whom are also workers – regarding unemployment benefits is very negative: 70 per cent of the interviewees think that unemployment benefits in Italy are insufficient (European Commission 2008: 30). In other words, at least with respect to unemployment protection benefits, Italian reforms have not been in line with the public opinion request for more protection, but rather much more in tune with the 'modernization' goals supported by both the European Commission and Italian experts who have had relevant governmental responsibilities over the past ten years.[7]

To sum up, the past years of employment policy reforms have clearly had a positive impact on employment and unemployment rates (which respectively went from 51.3 per cent in 1997 to 58.4 per cent in 2006, and from 11.8 per cent in 1997 to 6.2 per cent in 2007; OECD 2008; European Commission 2008), but if we look for an increase in freedom of choice for job-seekers we must draw a less positive picture, since we can register only a partial overall enhancement of opportunities (i.e. particularly with respect to vocational training) and increasing contract options for employers rather than for employees. Furthermore, if we look more generally at the preferences of the Italian population, we see that no policy solution adopted in the specific sub-field (unemployment benefits) has been considered particularly welcome by Italian citizens. Therefore, if we take a broad approach to the freedom of choice issue, the limited advances with respect to some employment services (vocational training, temporary work, etc.) are matched with a more general dissatisfaction with respect to employment protection policies, i.e. a reduction in freedom of choice has occurred since citizens would fully appreciate being able to choose adequate (with respect to their training) and secure jobs, rather than accepting flexible employment. Only employers have seen their freedom of choice widen with respect to employment contract selection.

Pensions Policy and Freedom of Choice

Unlike in employment policy, in the case of pensions the notion of free choice appears to be easier to analyse empirically since the presence of voluntary supplementary pension schemes could be a gross indicator of how 'free' the choice for an individual pension is. Indeed, the voluntary supplementary schemes offer an opportunity for citizens to choose pension 'products' offered by different providers – although it should not be taken for granted that such an opportunity is considered favourably by the citizens themselves, as we will illustrate in the following discussion. In other terms, whereas the compulsory pension scheme (publicly managed) does not provide any choice for citizens, the voluntary supplementary schemes and the development of a pension insurance market do provide greater choice opportunities for workers. From this standpoint, since the early 1990s Italian pension policies have been significantly reformed and the overall picture is today quite different from that in the past: due to the promotion of new privately managed supplementary pension schemes, Italian workers have currently a greater opportunity to select their own individual pension scheme. But how relevant was the 'freedom of choice' goal in the political discourse leading to the reforms?

If we take a close look at the arguments adopted by decision-makers in order to justify the reforms, we always fall into 'modernization', 'cost containment obligation' or 'equity' categories (Natali 2001; Ferrera and Gualmini 2004; Jessoula 2009). Looking in more detail, it is not by chance that the timing of the reforms is very similar to the employment policy case. Following the adoption of the Maastricht Treaty (1992), between 1992 and 1995 two major laws (Law 421/1992 and Law 335/1995) were adopted, changing some fundamental elements of the traditional pension policy configuration – previously characterized primarily by a public pillar and by an overall pensionrelated high public expenditure (Jessoula 2009). The first pension reform (Law 421/1992 and the related legislative decrees D. Lgs. 503/1992 and D. Legs. 124/1993) were aimed at changing pension regulations – i.e. making retirement schemes less 'generous' – and providing a new framework for supplementary occupational and private pensions. More specifically, eligibility conditions were tightened (retirement age was raised from 60 to 65 for male workers and from 55 to 60 for female workers) and the benefits were reduced. The second pension reform (Law 335/1995), among other relevant innovations, introduced a new contributory mechanism which changed the 'income maintenance' principle into an 'insurance' one (Jessoula 2009). In particular, one of the most remarkable aspects of the reform was the 'unfreezing' of the TFR – *Trattamento di fine rapporto* (End of work benefit), a 'second pillar pension scheme in disguise' (Ferrera and Gualmini 2004: 110), which consists in a sum set aside by employers on behalf of the employees which is then given to them either when they change jobs or when they retire. The 1992–3 reforms 'introduced a coordinated legal framework and fiscal incentives for the establishment of occupational supplementary funds and foresaw the possibility of diverting the TFR contributions into such new funds' (Ferrera and Gualmini 2004: 110). In other words, a freedom of choice was introduced with respect to the new opportunity to decide on the use of the TFR (about 7 per cent of the worker's gross salary).

The overall effect of these reforms is that the projected gross replacement rates of compulsory public retirement schemes will drop significantly over the next 50 years, although opening up new opportunities for the development of supplementary occupational schemes which – in the most optimistic forecasts – could almost entirely cover the losses connected to the public scheme decrease in generosity (table 2).

Even more clearly than in the case of other Italian welfare reforms, the pension policy changes were adopted in order to cope with the 'cost containment' imperatives which were channelled by European institutions, the main

Table 2

Projected gross replacement rates (%) for a private employee who retires at 60 with 35 years of contributions, 2000–2030

	2000	2010	2020	2030
Compulsory public pensions	67.3	67.1	56.0	49.6
Supplementary occupational pensions	0.0	4.7	9.4	14.5
Total	67.3	71.8	65.4	64.1

Source: Ministero del Welfare (2002: 11).

aim being to keep the Italian retirement schemes sustainable in the long term by controlling the overall public pensions expenditure (Ferrera and Gualmini 2004; Jessoula and Ferrera 2006). Again, if we look at the main arguments put forward by the key decision-makers in order to support their legislative proposals (and to negotiate with the trade unions, clearly key actors in this policy field due to the high percentage of 'unionized' retirees; Mania and Sateriale 2002), we find no sign of a 'freedom of choice' discourse. Indeed, we would not expect it in connection with the overall reform, but at least with reference to the supplementary pension schemes: one of the by-products of the policy innovation is that citizens may profit more from generous financial market gains (supplementary private schemes) than from fixed ones (public mandatory schemes). The necessary conditions for such virtuous outcome clearly are that individuals have to fund a second occupational and/or a third individual retirement scheme in order to profit from the opportunities offered by financial markets; the markets have to perform and be managed well – and in these times of harsh financial and economic crisis, doubts on this issue are particularly strong.

But how have citizens used this new possibility represented by the opportunity to join supplementary pension scheme programmes? Currently, less than 5 million workers have decided to profit from the new opportunities and invest in a supplementary scheme, whereas the remaining 18 million or so still prefer the more 'traditional' TFR (COVIP 2008: 14). Therefore, there is some evidence showing how the limited innovation provided implicitly by the reforms of the 1990s did not find much favour in workers' preferences. The future of supplementary pension schemes may change these figures, but probably the current financial and economic crisis may not constitute a strong incentive for new supplementary scheme subscriptions.

To resume, the development of pension policy shows how limited was the attention paid to the 'freedom of choice' argument, both in the policy formulation phase (no specific reference to the 'freedom of choice' argument made by key decision-makers) and policy implementation phase (limited use by workers of the new opportunities offered by the 'unfreezing' of the TFR). The reason for the total absence of any other argument different from the 'cost containment' one can be seen in the difficult conditions characterizing both the Italian political system and public debt in the early 1990s (Rossi 2007): in order to enter into the Eurozone, Italian governments needed to significantly reduce the Italian public debt (Verzichelli 1999) and prove to the European partners that such cuts would be long-lasting, not just cosmetic changes due to the threatening *vincolo esterno* [external link] represented by the European institutions (Dyson and Featherstone 1999). And it is not by chance that the key pension reforms were adopted by 'emergency' or 'technocratic' governments, i.e. governments that were formed primarily of ministers selected on the basis of their expertise rather than by virtue of their political affiliation. Therefore, any other reasons more grounded in political ideologies (such as a neo-liberal appraisal of a citizen's freedom and his freedom to choose) were virtually ignored by decision-makers. In fact, it could have been counterproductive for the government to relate to crucial political actors – such as the reluctant trade unions, which were of great relevance in supporting the reforms of the early 1990s (Mania and Sateriale 2002; Ferrera and Gualmini 2004) – that the reforms were promoted also in order to support a citizen's freedom of choice since the trade unions also have clearly an interest in limiting individual options and playing a political intermediation role.

Health-care Policy and Freedom of Choice

Health-care policy is probably the one best suited to be studied for the analysis of freedom of choice patterns. Indeed, in the Italian case, and especially in some regions such as Lombardy (Colombo 2008), the evolution of health care is very interesting with respect to the development of 'freedom of choice' – at least from a political discourse perspective – but also in this case we shall see that other stronger arguments were made in order to support reform. After the 1978 reform, the universalistic Italian health-care system offered very limited opportunities for a citizen to choose choice within the public SSN – *Sistema sanitario nazionale* (National health system), a system almost entirely based on public health-care services. To be sure, citizens could choose (limited) private health-care services, but they had to pay for them or – just as in other welfare models – buy private insurance in order to be protected from health risks. The two main reforms of the 1990s (the 1992–3 so-called 'reform of the reform', based on the legislative decrees 502/1992 and 517/1993, and the decree 229/1999) were aimed, on the one hand, at finding a better equilibrium among the various institutions involved in health-care policies (primarily the state administration and the regional authorities; Maino 2001; Ferrera and Gualmini 2004; Pizzuti 2007; Neri 2008), and, on the other hand, at making the system more efficient by keeping under control its overall cost (Fattore 1999) which had increased from 5.6 per cent of Italian GDP in 1997 to 6.8 per cent in 2005 (Eurostat 2008: 77). As in the case of pensions, new business opportunities were offered to companies interested in entering (or consolidating their position in) the health-care sector. The Legislative Decree 502/1992 increased the opportunities for private providers to be accredited by the national health-care system (i.e. providers authorized – and monitored – by a public body to 'sell' health-care services to citizens) and therefore citizens currently have in principle more freedom of choice in selecting their hospitals

Paolo R. Graziano

Table 3

Public health expenditure as percentage of total health
expenditure

	1990	1995	2001	2006
Italy	79.1	71.9	75.8	73.0

Source: Pizzuti (2007: 112).

and – to a certain extent – publicly funded doctors (*medici di base*). Furthermore, freedom of choice has remained with respect to the additional services which are not covered by the national health system – although these are very limited due to the proportion of private health care expenditure compared to the public one (table 3).

Nevertheless, these two potentially innovative opportunities for increasing citizens' choice options were not fully exploited in their political discourses by the national decision-makers. Furthermore, one of the major changes – decentralization – increased the role of regional decision-makers and in only some cases (where evidence of 'freedom of choice' enhancement can be found, as in the case of the Lombardy Region: Colombo 2008) may we detect a significant increase in the overall choice opportunities for citizens. In fact, currently there is no national health-care system but different regional health-care systems co-funded nationally (Maino 2001; Pizzuti 2007; Neri 2008). Therefore, a significant territorial differentiation in health-care protection is emerging in Italy. Stefano Neri identifies three regional health-care models which are very useful also with respect to the degree of 'freedom of choice' implied. The first model (the Lombardy or 'competition' model) is character-ized by open competition among health-care providers and a limited coordi-nation role in the hands of the regional public administration. In the words of Neri: '[In Lombardy] a great emphasis is put on the freedom of choice principle with regard to the health-care service provider ... The citizen[s] can freely choose any public or accredited private preferred health-care service provider' (2008: 106). In other regions, such as Emilia Romagna or Veneto, another model ('integration' model) can be detected: in this one, coordination and programming tasks are performed by the regional authorities, whereas individual freedom in the selection of health-care service providers is not as wide as in the 'competition' model. The third ('residualincremental') model – which can be found in Southern regions – is a mix of the above-mentioned models in which bureaucratic programming is combined with some competi-tion ingredients.

Therefore, the picture is quite mixed with respect to health-care services: in some Italian regions the degree of freedom of choice has increased signifi-cantly (primarily via the accreditation system, such as in the Lombardy case) whereas in others fewer options for citizens in need of health-care services are

72

guaranteed, due to the presence of a strong programming and, to a certain degree, management role of the regional government (for example, Emilia Romagna).

To be sure, health-care policy has followed the same cost containment imperative as many other social policies, although in this case the key concern was not primarily to reduce costs *per se* but to share cost responsibilities with the sub-national public authorities and set national targets in order to keep overall public expenditure under control (Maino 2003; Pizzuti 2008; Neri 2008). Therefore, the implementation of the reforms left space for manoeuvre in the hands of the regional authorities which, in some cases, did increase the choice options for citizens in the selection of health-care service providers. To conclude, the illustration of the recent evolution of health-care political discourse and policy shows that as a by-product of the increased regional competences, some citizens – in some regions – have been benefiting from more freedom of choice due to the favourable political preferences and public policies of certain regional governments. If we look at the national level, however, no national rigid prescription was passed on to the regions, although coordination tasks still remain anchored at the central level: Italy is currently characterized by the co-presence of different models of health-care protection that offer quite differentiated 'freedom of choice' for citizens, which may increasingly differ in function of their territorial location, but the main push for recent health-care reforms – at least at the national level – can be found in more relevant 'cost containment' or 'cost sharing' imperatives.

More (Limited) Freedom, but Less (National) Social Citizenship: The Italian Lesson

Before drawing a cross-policy conclusion and answering the main question raised by this chapter (i.e., have recent welfare state reforms been grounded in a political discourse supporting the increase of citizens' 'freedom of choice'?), we need to briefly recapitulate our main findings. First, over the past fifteen years the rhetoric of free choice has entered into the political debate and on to the political agenda of several leading political parties, but very limited evidence concerning the relevance of this factor can be found in the analysis of specific national welfare state reforms (employment, pensions, health care). Second, in the various policies analysed, we did find some reinforcement of freedom of choice for citizens but such a goal has been reached only as a by-product of other goals perceived to be more relevant (modernization, cost containment, etc.) and in a differentiated way with respect to the various policies (and regional territories). With regard to health-care policy and to a certain extent employment policy, in some regions reforms have been sustained by a clear 'freedom of choice' rhetoric but there is no convergence towards a 'national' standard which further reinforces choice options for citizens. Therefore, as the literature and the policy documents clearly demonstrate, we are moving towards regional models – with the clear exception of pensions – where the 'ideologies' of welfare are quite differentiated. Third, because of the cost containment imperative, recent Italian reforms have recalibrated the welfare state by reducing coverage (for example, pension replacement rates), limiting protection (for example, by increasing flexibility in employment policies) and increasing welfare costs for citizens (for example, the increasing expansion of the use of 'tickets' for selected health-care services which are *ad hoc* contributions paid by patients). To sum up: over the past years a significant recalibration, if not a reduction, of Italian (national) social citizenship has occurred.

In comparative terms, unlike other welfare state models or regimes, the Italian case has been only marginally involved in a coherent and nationally developed increase in the choice options for citizens. The main reason for this can be found in the cost containment and modernization goals pursued by both centre-left and centre-right governments over recent years. To be sure, neo-liberal claims, centred on the relevance of providing more freedom of choice for citizens, have been increasingly visible in the political campaigns and political agendas, but surprisingly absent in the specific arguments made for Italian welfare state reforms. Furthermore, since the costs needed to be contained, the overall social protection of Italian citizens (especially of the elderly) has been reduced. Finally, the decentralization process of welfare services (in particular with respect to employment and health care) is opening new differentiated forms of 'choice' welfare, thus endangering the future development of a coherent and comprehensive national welfare state in Italy.

Acknowledgements

I would like to thank Matteo Jessoula for very useful discussions and comments on the ideas developed in this chapter, and Susan Lovegrove for vital linguistic assistance.

Notes

1. For recent UK developments in selected policy areas, see Greener and Powell (2008).
2. For the definition and relevance of the concept of political discourse with respect to welfare state politics, see Schmidt (2002).
3. Silvio Berlusconi, TV declaration, 26 January 1994.
4. At: www.partitodemocratico.it/allegatidef/Programma%20PD45315.pdf, p. 4.
5. Standard workers are characterized by a full-time contract and a continuous employment relationship, typically with one employer.
6. In fact, the most evident implication of the reform is that currently employers have more freedom to select employment contracts since the general contract negotiations made by trade unions only rarely affect 'precarious' contracts, and therefore the worker has very limited bargaining power (i.e. freedom of choice) with respect to their employment contract conditions.
7. For further details on the role of the European Union and experts in recent Italian employment policy reforms, see Graziano (2004).

References

Ascoli, U. (ed.) (1985), *Welfare State all'italiana*, Roma-Bari: Laterza.
Blomqvist, P. (2004), The choice revolution: privatization of Swedish welfare services in the 1990s, *Social Policy & Administration*, 38, 2: 139–55.

Boeri, T. (2000), *Uno stato asociale* [An asocial state], Roma-Bari: Laterza.

Colombo, A. (2008), The 'Lombardy model': subsidiarity-informed regional governance, *Social Policy & Administration*, 42, 2: 177–96.

Cotta, M. and Isernia, P. (eds) (1996), *Il gigante dai piedi d'argilla* [The clay-footed giant], Bologna: Il Mulino.

Cotta, M. and Verzichelli, L. (2007), *Political Institutions in Italy*, Oxford: Oxford University Press.

COVIP (2008), *Relazione Anno 2008*, Roma: COVIP.

Dyson, K. and Featherstone, K. (1999), *The Road to Maastricht: Negotiating Economic and Monetary Union*, Oxford: Oxford University Press.

Esping-Andersen, G. (1990), *The Three Worlds of Welfare Capitalism*, New York: Policy Press.

European Commission (2008), *Standard Eurobarometer Survey*, No. 69, Luxembourg: EC.

Eurostat (2008), *European Social Statistics: Social Protection, Expenditure and Receipts*, Luxembourg: Eurostat.

Fattore, G. (1999), Clarifying the scope of Italian NHS coverage. Is it feasible? Is it desirable? *Health Policy*, 50, 1–2: 123–42.

Ferrera, M. (1984), *Il welfare state in Italia*, Bologna: Il Mulino.

Ferrera, M. (1996), The 'Southern model' of welfare in Social Europe, *Journal of European Social Policy*, 6, 1: 17–37.

Ferrera, M. (1998), *Le trappole del welfare* [Welfare traps], Bologna: Il Mulino.

Ferrera, M. (ed.) (2005), *Welfare State Reform in Southern Europe: Fighting Poverty and Social Exclusion in Italy, Spain, Portugal and Greece*, New York: Routledge.

Ferrera, M. and Gualmini, E. (2004), *Rescued by Europe? Social and Labour Market Reforms from Maastricht to Berlusconi*, Amsterdam: Amsterdam University Press.

Ferrera, M. and Hemerijck, A. (2003), Recalibrating European Welfare Regimes. In J. Zeitlin and D. Trubek (eds), *Governing Work and Welfare in a New Economy: European and American Experiments*, Oxford: Oxford University Press, pp. 88–128.

Graziano, P. (2004), *Europeizzazione e Politiche Pubbliche Italiane: Coesione e Lavoro a Confronto* [Europeanization and Italian public policy: cohesion and labour compared], Bologna: Il Mulino.

Graziano, P. (2007), Adapting to the European Employment Strategy? Continuity and change in recent Italian employment policy, *International Journal of Comparative Labour Law and Industrial Relations*, 23, 4: 543–65.

Graziano, P., Madama, I. and Jessoula, M. (2008), The emergence of mid-sider workers? The effects of the Italian employment policy configuration on non-unionized workers. Paper presented at the RECWOWE Seminar on 'The Politics of Flexicurity', Edinburgh, 13–14 December.

Greener, I. and Powell, M. (2008), The evolution of choice policies in the UK: housing, education and health policy, *Journal of Social Policy*, 38, 1: 63–81.

Gualmini, E. (1998), *La politica del lavoro* [Labour policy], Bologna: Il Mulino.

Immergut, E. M., Anderson, K. M. and Schultze, I. (eds) (2006), *Handbook of Western Pension Politics*, Oxford: Oxford University Press.

Jessoula, M. (2009), *La politica pensionistica* [Pension policy], Bologna: Il Mulino.

Jessoula, M. and Ferrera, M. (2006), Italy: A Narrow Gate for Path-shift. In K. Anderson, E. Immergut and I. Schulze (eds), *Handbook of West European Pension Politics*, Oxford: Oxford University Press.

Legnante, G. and Sani, S. (2002), La campagna più lunga [The longest campaign]. In R. D'Alimonte and S. Bartolini (eds), *Maggioritario finalmente?* [Majority at last?] Bologna: Il Mulino.

Legnante, G. and Sani, S. (2007), Campagna elettorale e sondaggi [Electoral campaign and soundings]. In R. D'Alimonte and A. Chiaramente (eds), *Proporzionale ma non solo* [Proportional but not only], Bologna: Il Mulino.

Maino, F. (2001), *La politica sanitaria in Italia* [Health policy in Italy], Bologna: Il Mulino.

Maino, F. (2003), L'europeizzazione della sanità: la politica sanitaria italiana tra patti esterni e patti interni [The Europeanization of health: Italian health policy between external and internal pacts]. In S. Fabbrini (ed.), *L'europeizzazione dell'Italia: L'impatto dell'Unione europea nelle istituzioni e le politiche italiane* [The Europeanization of Italy: the impact of the European Union on Italian institutions and politics], Roma-Bari: Laterza, pp. 164–89.

Mania, R. and G. Sateriale (2002), *Relazioni pericolose: sindacati e politica dopo la concertazione* [Dangerous relations: unions and policy after consultation], Bologna: Il Mulino.

Marshall, T. H. (1950), *Citizenship and Social Class and Other Essays*, Cambridge: Cambridge University Press.

Ministero del Welfare (2001), *Libro Bianco sul mercato del lavoro in Italia* [White Paper on the labour market in Italy], Roma.

Ministero del Welfare (2002), *Report on National Strategies for Future Pension Systems*, Roma.

Morel, N. (2007), From subsidiarity to 'free choice': child-and elder-policy reforms in France, Belgium, Germany and the Netherlands, *Social Policy & Administration*, 41, 6: 618–37.

Natali, D. (2001). La ridefinizione del welfare state contemporaneo: la riforma delle pensioni in Francia e in Italia [The redefinition of the contemporary welfare state: the reform of pensions in France and Italy]. Phd dissertation, EUI-Florence.

Neri, S. (2008), La costruzione dei Servizi Sanitari regionali e la governance del sistema sanitario [The construction of regional health services and the governance of the health system], *La Rivista delle Politiche Sociali*, 3: 97–114.

OECD (2008), *Social Expenditure Database*, Paris: OECD.

Pirrone, S. and Sestito, P. (2006), *Disoccupati in Italia* [Unemployed in Italy], Bologna: Il Mulino.

Pizzuti, F. R. (ed.) (2007), *Rapporto sullo stato sociale 2007* [Report on the welfare state 2007], Novara: De Agostini – UTET.

Pizzuti, F. R. (ed.) (2008), *Rapporto sullo stato sociale 2008* [Report on the welfare state 2008], Novara: De Agostini – UTET.

Rossi, S. (2007), *La politica economica italiana 1968–2007* [Italian economic policy 1968–2007], Roma-Bari: Laterza.

Samek Lodovici, M. and Semenza, R. (2008), The Italian case: from employment regulation to welfare reforms? *Social Policy & Administration*, 42, 2: 160–76.

Schmidt, V. (2002), Does discourse matter in the politics of welfare state adjustment? *Comparative Political Studies*, 35, 2: 168–93.

Segatti, P. (1995), I programmi elettorali e il ruolo dei mass media [Electoral programmes and the role of the mass media]. In S. Bartolini and R. D'Alimonte, *Maggioritario ma non troppo* [Majoritarian but not too much], Bologna: Il Mulino.

Thomson, S. and Mossialos, E. (2006), Choice of public or private health insurance: learning from the experience of Germany and the Netherlands, *Journal of European Social Policy*, 16, 4: 315–27.

Treu, T. (2001), *Politiche del lavoro: Insegnamenti di un decennio* [Labour policies: lessons of a decade], Bologna: Il Mulino.

Verzichelli, L. (1999), *La politica di bilancio* [Fiscal policy], Bologna: Il Mulino.

6

The 'Consumer Principle' in the Care of Elderly People: Free Choice and Actual Choice in the German Welfare State

Melanie Eichler and Birgit Pfau-Effinger

Introduction

In the last decade, a restructuring of welfare state policies towards care for elderly people took place in many European societies, as a reaction to new challenges. Demographic change has contributed to an extension of the need for long-term care for the elderly. Women, who were traditionally the main providers of long-term care in the framework of the family, were to a greater extent integrated into the labour market and therefore available as providers to a lesser degree than had previously been the case. Because of such changes, there was an increasing demand for public or publicly financed long-term care. Together with this development, in the framework of an overall trend towards individualization and democratization in European societies, the demand for a high quality of care and the autonomy and participation of those who are in need of care and their relatives has also grown. As a reaction to such challenges, the public supply of long-term care was extended in many European welfare states, and in part new rights to choose between different forms of care provision were introduced for elderly people.

At the same time, a restructuring of policies towards elderly care took place that was based on a paradigm shift towards the strengthening of economic principles and a new emphasis on 'choice' and the role of the market for the provision of elderly care, and on efficiency as a new main welfare value. Accordingly, the introduction of new welfare markets, in which non-profit and market-based providers compete, of elements of new public management and of new Fordist principles into professional care work were main elements of the restructuring process (Bode 2005; Clarke 2006; Lundsgaard 2006; Rostgaard 2006; Vabo 2006; Theobald *et al.* 2007; Pavolini and Ranci 2008; Pfau-Effinger *et al.* 2008). In Germany, the importance of elements such as the market and 'consumer choice' in the organization of care has been bolstered by the Long-Term Care Insurance Act (*Pflegeversicherungsgesetz*; SGB XI) that was implemented in 1995/6.

In this way the choice between publicly funded family care, publicly funded professional care by ambulant care services and a combination of the two was introduced for those in need of care who wished to continue to live in their own household in old age. In addition, they can also choose between various providers of care: service agencies run by local authorities or non-profit organizations, as well as commercial providers.

What is surprising, however, is that the majority of those in need of care and their families do not use the options offered by ambulant care at all. Instead, the care for which payments from the long-term care insurance fund are claimed is to an overwhelming extent carried out exclusively by family members. In comparison to the time before the introduction of long-term care insurance, the proportion of those in need of care who are exclusively cared for by family members has not even substantially decreased. This chapter asks about the causes for this. Why do the majority of those in need of care not accept the options offered by diverse types of ambulant care, or not even a combined solution, instead continuing to choose exclusively the traditional model of care, specifically care by family members?

We argue that elderly persons in need of care often do not act as autonomous actors who choose between different offers on welfare markets. Instead, the decision is in many cases taken in a complex family context. Also, choice decisions in the context of 'consumer choice' cannot simply be traced back to material motives in the sense of a narrow understanding of 'rational choice'. Instead, cultural factors also contribute to the explanation to a significant extent, as we hope to show in what follows.

The first section discusses the ways in which the introduction of the Long-Term Care Insurance Act in Germany in the mid-1990s opened up new possibilities for choice in household care between family care and various forms of publicly financed care by care services. In the second section we show how the actual decision on the part of those in need of care and their family members with regard to care after the introduction of long-term care insurance has developed. In the third section, current approaches to explanation in the literature are discussed. In the fourth part we demonstrate that cultural factors have also made an important contribution to the fact that the proportion of those in need of care who are exclusively cared for by family members is still so high in Germany.

Care Policy and the Expansion of Choice in Germany with the Introduction of the Long-term Care Insurance Act 1995/1996

Until the early 1990s, the care of elderly people in Germany had essentially been organized as unpaid family care, and for this reason the classification of the German welfare state in this respect as a 'conservative welfare regime' in Esping-Andersen (1990, 1999) and as a 'political regime strongly oriented towards the male breadwinner' in Lewis (1992) is fully accurate. Care in care homes, on the other hand, played a secondary role in comparison, and the proportion of ambulant professional care by care services was also relatively low (Alber and Schölkopf 1999).

With the Long-Term Care Insurance Act implemented in 1995 and 1996, care of elderly people was for the first time in Germany defined as a task for the central state, and a new social insurance was established that financed a universal basic provision for those in need of care on the basis of contributions from everyone in gainful employment. An important goal of this was to make it possible for those in need of care to live a self-determined life in a private household and to claim care from family members and social networks or ambulant care by professional care services for this purpose.

If those in need of care decide to be cared for by family members, these family members receive a certain very low payment for their care work within the framework of long-term care insurance, which is defined as 'compensation for effort' – analogously to voluntary work; the expression also originates from this sector (cf. Pfau-Effinger *et al.* 2009). This is considerably less than the payment made by the long-term care insurance fund if the person in need of care opts for ambulant care by care services. In this case, the size of insurance payments differs according to which of the three 'care levels' the person in need of care has been assigned to, and thus according to the extent of that person's requirement for care. If a person in need of care opts for care by an ambulant care service, the long-term care insurance fund pays a lump sum ('benefits in kind') to the care service. This should cover a particular period of time for care per week. Benefits in kind of €420 (care level 1), €980 (care level 2) or €1,470 (care level 3) are guaranteed (Deutscher Bundestag 2007: SGB XI). In comparison with professional care services, family members involved in care receive a considerably lower sum for the same extent of care. It is also not paid directly to them by the long-term care insurance fund but by the person in need of care – this constitutes a system of 'routed wages' in the sense used by Ungerson (2005). Payments for family members involved in care are from €215 per month (care level 1), to €420 per month (care level 2) and €675 per month (care level 3). Compared to the average amount of time a private carer spends on care (Schneekloth 2005b), this corresponds to a payment of between roughly 2 and 3 euros per hour. In addition, family members involved in care also receive entitlement to pension insurance (care level 2 and 3).[1]

On the basis of the financing of ambulant professional care by the long-term care insurance fund, the emergence of a broad sector of publicly financed providers in the field of ambulant care was encouraged. At the same time, economic principles were considerably strengthened in the social field of the care of elderly people. As a basis for the organization of care in the ambulant care services, principles of market, of competition and of efficiency were introduced with the Act. Quasi-market-like 'welfare markets' were established, in which various types of providers, also including companies in the private sector, compete for contracts (Backhaus-Maul and Olk 1997; Schmidt and Klie 1998; Schulz-Nieswandt 2002; Schmidt 2002; Bode 2005).

On the basis of these changes in the institutional framework for care, the autonomy of those in need of care has tended to be strengthened, since elderly people can now release themselves from the relationship of dependence in which they are placed by family care through opting for ambulant professional care. Care for family members involved in care often leads to massive overloading. The work requires round-the-clock availability of the carer and can often lead to a feeling of overwork and social isolation, especially when caring for a family member who requires extensive care (Motel-Klingebiel 2002; Mischke and Meyer 2008).

Development of the Structure of Care of Elderly People

In view of the far-reaching changes in the welfare state framework for the care of elderly people that the Long-Term Care Insurance Act brought with it, it was to be expected that the contribution of ambulant care services to the provision of elderly care would be substantially extended. Policy-makers like Norbert Bluem, the Minister of Social Affairs of the Christian Democratic Party (CDU), predicted that more than 400,000 new jobs would be created after the introduction of the new legislation (Pabst 1999). It is therefore surprising that the structures of care have changed only comparatively little since its introduction.

According to representative censuses, the care of frail elderly people who live in private households is still carried out, in by far the largest proportion of cases, exclusively by family members, as it was before the introduction of the Long-Term Care Insurance Act. The percentage in this group had reached 79.6 at the time of the introduction of long-term care insurance. Following this, the percentage fell from 79.6 in 1996 to 71.5 in 2006, but not nearly to the extent that could have been expected and that was actually expected on the part of politicians (Pabst 1999; Schneekloth 2005a; Deutscher Bundestag 2008). In other words, more than two-thirds of those elderly people defined as needing care in long-term care insurance terms, who are cared for in private households, are still cared for exclusively by family members (cf. figure 1).

As figure 1 makes clear, the possibility that was created with the introduction of long-term care insurance – to claim options of care services in addition to or instead of family care and to receive payments from the long-term care insurance fund for this – has so far been comparatively little used. The proportion of households in which care is carried out exclusively by care services has increased by a mere 4 percentage points (from 8.9 to 13.2 per cent) within the ten years following the introduction of long-term care insurance (1996–2006). Furthermore, only a relatively low percentage, 15.3 in 2006 (in 1996, 11.4 per cent), opted for a combination of care by family members and care by care services.

Accordingly, the number of jobs which were created also remained far below the expected level (Pabst 1999). These data demonstrate impressively that the proportions of the various forms of care in the household for elderly people have only marginally changed. Although professional care in private households has increased slightly over the last decade, the family still remains the most important provider of elderly care in Germany today.

Figure 1

Organization of home-based elder care in Germany, 1991–2006 (%)

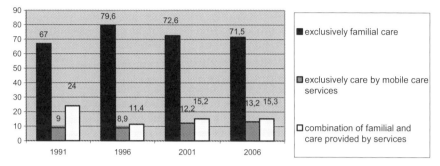

Source: For 1991: Schneekloth (2005a). For 1996–2006: Deutscher Bundestag (2008), and the authors' calculation.

Discussion of Possible Explanatory Factors in the Literature

It must now be explained why those in need of care and their family members continue to choose the traditional solution of care by family members despite the large expansion of possibilities between family care and care by various providers in the area of ambulant care services.

Christiane Dienel, who has carried out international comparative studies of the structures of care, argues that deficits in the care infrastructure are a possible explanation for the high proportions of family care in some European countries (Dienel 2007). For Germany, however, this argument is less applicable. To all intents and purposes, a sufficient infrastructure for care exists on the basis of a variety of ambulant care services operated by welfare organizations, local authorities and businesses, and whose care is to a large extent measured to professional standards.

According to another argument, which is particularly adduced by representatives of a 'rational choice' approach, primarily economic considerations are of decisive importance in choosing which form of care to opt for. The basis for this type of argument is provided by the 'household economy' approach of Gary Becker (Becker 1993). Becker argues that decision processes in the private household are centred on economic cost–benefit considerations. The aim is to maximize benefit for the individual. According to this argument, care benefit payments guaranteed by the long-term care insurance fund, which could be gained over the same period of time, could provide a financial incentive for family members and acquaintances to take on the care of a closely associated person rather than transferring this to ambulant care services.

In the current case, this argument is rather less applicable. From the perspective of family members who take on the care of frail elderly members of their family on the basis of the cash benefits provided through long-term care insurance, these payments can never compete with the income from formal gainful employment. The size of cash benefits (around €2–3 per hour) is far below the hourly rate that one can expect to be paid on average in formal gainful employment. Care by family members is thus generally not a financially attractive alternative. The argument based on economic incentive is therefore unconvincing.

Moreover, it might be assumed that not only financial considerations but also the wish to secure one's autonomy plays an important role for the decision of elderly people in need of care between different options. In this regard, care by care agencies is more favourable, as the scope for decision-making on the part of the person in need of care can be much higher in this type of care than when being cared for by a relative. This is also the finding of a qualitative study based on interviews carried out by Heusinger and Klünder between 1999 and 2004 (Heusinger and Klünder 2005: 174).[2]

Altogether, the currently available explanatory approaches are thus not sufficient to explain why the proportion of frail elderly people who are exclusively cared for by relatives still remains so high despite the important changes in the welfare state framework and the massive increase in the spectrum of provision of ambulant care services.

The Contribution of Cultural Factors to the Explanation

We argue that cultural factors contribute significantly to explaining why people in need of care and their family members generally continue to choose the traditional solution of care by family members despite the variety of possibilities for choice available to them. These cultural factors primarily lie in

- the orientation of the population towards traditional cultural values that give priority to family care; and
- the mismatch between the attitudes towards the characteristics of 'good care' dominant among the population, on the one hand, and the strong orientation of care by care services towards economic criteria, on the other hand.

To support our argument, in the following we evaluate data from several representative surveys on care and present the results of a qualitative study we carried out from 2004 to 2005 in private households in four regions of East and West Germany.[3]

The importance of the cultural value of family care in Germany

The society of the Federal Republic of Germany has traditionally been a 'home care society' in which childcare and care of the elderly by family members in the private household are held in particularly high regard. In the West German 'gender arrangement', the family model of the 'housewife marriage' formed the cultural context and the basis for the institutional framing of the family by the welfare state in the 1950s, 1960s and 1970s. The model provided for a male family breadwinner to secure the family's income on the basis of his gainful employment and for his wife, who was not in gainful employment, to look after the housework and family support and care (Ostner 1998; Pfau-Effinger 2004). Family care is still seen in both parts of Germany as the 'best' form of care for elderly people, on the basis of a high estimation of the cultural values of solidarity and moral responsibility between family members. In line with these similarities in attitudes, the proportion of elderly people who are exclusively cared for by family members is also rather similar in both parts of Germany.

A representative survey across Germany by Runde, Giese and Stierle (2003) on the effects of long-term care insurance, carried out for the first time in 1996/7 and a second time in 2002 in care households, showed that the family members of those in need of care are seen as having a moral responsibility to take on the long-term care of their relatives (figure 2).

The answer statements in the survey aim to identify the degree of moral responsibility towards long-term care for family members. The majority of the surveyed family members involved in care declared in 1997 that they saw themselves as morally responsible for the care of relatives who were in need of long-term care (57.8 per cent). Marriage partners in particular were judged by the majority to have a right to receive long-term care from their partner (71.1 per cent). The proportion of those who assumed that children had a responsibility to care for their parents, on the other hand, was slightly lower (55 per cent). The moral responsibility of family members as an

Figure 2

Attitudes to the participation of family members in elder care in the context of long-term care insurance

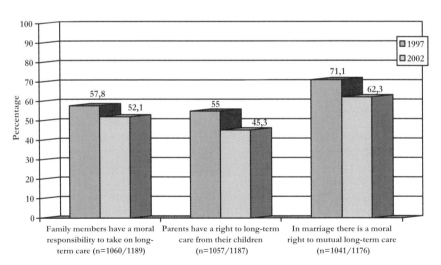

Source: Cross-sectional comparison of 1997 and 2002, survey of service recipients of a major German health insurance/care insurance company, agreement in percent (cf. Runde *et al.* 2003).

unquestioned norm has lost importance with the turn of the millennium. This can be seen on the basis of the figure: in 2002, only a minority of 45.3 per cent viewed children as having a duty to take on the long-term care of their elderly family members, and a considerably lower proportion than before (62.3 per cent compared to 71.1 per cent) thought that marriage partners had a responsibility to provide mutual long-term care. This change was probably a result of the increasing possibility of claiming entitlement to ambulant care services, which was improved by the Long-Term Care Insurance Act. However, those who believed that the family had a duty to take on the long-term care of elderly family members were still in the majority in 2002 (52.1 per cent).

These cultural values, which are widespread among the population, also form the cultural context and background for the decision of family members to take on the long-term care of relatives. This is shown, for example, by the representative survey carried out by Eisen and Mager between 2001 and 2003 in long-term care households in the state of Hessen (cf. Mager 2007). Family members involved in care were asked which reasons had been decisive in their choice to look after the long-term care of their relatives. Those surveyed primarily cited cultural values of solidarity and moral responsibility between family members. For example, three-quarters (77.4 per cent) of those surveyed agreed with the statement 'It goes without saying for me to take on the long-term care of a family member', and the majority of those surveyed (53.4 per cent) also agreed with the statement 'I feel personally responsible for carrying out long-term care' (Mager 2007: 4).[4] Financial reasons do enter into the decision to take on long-term care, but they are of lesser significance. The study shows that only 11 per cent of those surveyed agreed with the statement 'The financial compensation I receive for long-term care provides me with additional income'. Moreover, in the context of securing inheritance, only 10 per cent of those surveyed agreed with the statement that 'inheritance of the family's assets can be secured in this way' (Mager 2007: 4). Those findings show that cultural attitudes to values regarding the responsibility of the family for long-term care are the key reason that care is often carried out exclusively by family members (Mager and Eisen 2002; Mager 2007).

Discrepancies regarding attitudes to 'good care'

The findings of a qualitative empirical study show that contradictions with regard to the definition of 'good care' contribute to explaining why the option to choose care provided by long-term care agencies is only used by relatively few people (Eichler 2005).

The study was based on 33 partially structured interviews carried out with women who are carrying out family care (23 respondents) and elderly people in need of care (10 respondents) in 2004 and 2005. These were all private households in which an elderly person drew benefits from the care insurance fund and in which care was carried out either completely by a family member or an acquaintance on the basis of cash benefits (13 cases) or by a family member or an acquaintance with the support of professional services (11 cases). The majority (16 surveyed carers) were the wives of men in need of long-term care; seven carers were daughters of a parent in need of long-term care.

The women surveyed were asked about their motives for taking on long-term care, about the organization of care, about their work situation in the context of care and about the importance of payments for care. The completely transcribed interviews were analysed using Mayring's (1997) method for 'qualitative content analysis'.

The transcripts were completely anonymized. All names of interview partners given in the following have been changed in advance. On the basis of the research questions, we developed a system of categories, which we drew upon as a coding scheme for the evaluation of the interviews. The evaluation of the interviews was computer-aided, with the help of MAXQDA (Eichler 2005).

The results of the interviews show that long-term care as it is offered by the care services often does not correspond to the expectations of 'good care' in care households, and that this is a further factor contributing to the one-sided preference for family care in many care households. The term 'quality' can be viewed as a construct of multiple perspectives, which is fulfilled differently from the perspective of each actor (Fthenakis and Textor 1998). There can therefore be differences between groups of actors in attitudes to what constitutes a good quality of care (Pfau-Effinger *et al.* 2007, 2008).

Attitudes to a 'good quality' of care in care households. In the foreground of the attitudes of those in need of care and their family members to what constitutes 'good care' was what can be described as 'socially embedded' care.

The need for long-term care presents a particularly difficult situation for many elderly people. For one thing, dealing with the deterioration of one's own state of health is difficult to accept, and for another, getting used to being supported by a third party often constitutes a substantial readjustment (Schütte 2007). As was clear from the interviews in our study, care is a very private and to some extent also extremely intimate matter. Trust in the carer is therefore viewed as the fundamental basis for a good care relationship. A stable, continuous care relationship is thus seen as a central precondition for the development of a trusting social relationship between the person in need of care and the carer. While care by a family member or other close acquaintance is generally already based on a relationship of trust, trust in an unknown professional carer must first develop.

This finding is also supported by the data from the representative survey by Runde *et al.* (2003). In 2002, some 75.5 per cent of those surveyed stated that a good relationship with the carer entered into the decision when choosing a given form of care – almost as high a proportion as in 1997 (76.6 per cent) (Runde *et al.* 2003: 52).[5]

The discrepancy between the expectations in long-term care households and the conditions of ambulant care. The manner in which care by a care service is carried out often does not correspond to the notions of 'good care' that are dominant among care households.

The provisions of the Long-Term Care Insurance Act, which forms the framework for ambulant care, contribute significantly to this. The Act stipulates that the care services should carry out their work according to criteria of efficiency and a strict relationship between payment and services provided. They also compete for the public contracts on the care market on this basis. Care work in homes and by ambulant care services is normalized and standardized for this. A clearly defined relationship was introduced between payment and services provided; it is possible to speak in this context of a 'Taylorization of care' (cf. also Knijn 2000; Pfau-Effinger *et al.* 2007).

The organization of care by care services thus exhibits certain characteristics which make it unattractive as an alternative to family care from the perspective of a considerable proportion of those in need of care and their family members. These characteristics include:

- the frequent change of care staff;
- the predetermined time of day for daily care; and
- the high speed with which care is carried out.

The *frequent change of care staff* is seen as a hindrance to the development of a basis of trust.

> '*They, they trust you, it's always the same person who comes to them, whereas if they use a care service, the, um, the carers change practically every four hours. (hm) You always get someone new coming. And each one has a, a different approach, and each different carer does it differently. (hm, hm, yes) And that's actually terrible for these people, don't you think?*' (Mrs Quick; caring wife)

In these circumstances, trust and a social connection between the professional carer and the person in need of care can only be built up with difficulty. This was named by a large proportion of the care households surveyed as a key reason for not (also) drawing upon an ambulant care service.

In addition, the organization of work on the basis of *predetermined time of day for daily care* by the ambulant services is also seen as stopping the professional carers from being able to serve the needs of the person in need of care appropriately. This is shown, for instance, by the following interview extract:

> [in her justification for why she gave up additional care by ambulant services] '*It's just that, in the morning, to be plain about it, you can't go to the toilet on command. Or to the commode ... The care service washes you, you're washed really snappily, according to their timetable. I mean, I wouldn't want to be washed like that. And then you go back to bed and the care service goes away again. And then? I need to go again, I really need to go again. And who has to deal with it? The family.*' (Mrs Lang; caring wife)

The need for care, then, often arises irregularly and at unpredictable times. An organization of care on the basis of fixed visiting times, as is normal in the care services, is thus not appropriate from the perspective of care households.

The *high speed with which care is carried out* and, linked to this also, the short duration of stay of the carers from ambulant care services, are also seen as reducing the quality of care. The assignment of care service personnel to work, which is oriented towards an efficient form of care and the institutionally stipulated relationship between work and pay, is restricted to those tasks designated as 'necessary'. According to the opinions of those surveyed, this type of care conflicts fundamentally with the requirements of those in need of care, for whom a slower service and time for a conversation would be important.

Overall, the provisions of the ambulant care services are, in the opinion of those surveyed, not compatible in several essential aspects with the requirements of those in need of care for flexible, socially embedded care that meets their needs. The restricted definition of 'care' in the Long-Term Care Insurance Act, which shapes the concept of care among the care services, is also important for this. The definition limits care to medical and nursing provision, with physical care in the foreground. The emotional and social aspects of the care relationship, on the other hand, are largely excluded. This stands in conflict with the orientation towards a holistic care relationship in care households.

In consequence, this leads to those in need of care and their family members in many cases continuing to opt exclusively for family care instead of choosing ambulant care or, at least, combination solutions in which family care is supplemented by ambulant care. Family care is often seen as the type of care that is more appropriate to the temporal needs of those in need of care and their requirements for care to be socially embedded, rather than ambulant care by care services, and therefore family care is seen as the only guarantor of 'good care'.

Overall it is evident that there are discrepancies in the definition of what is understood as a 'good quality of care' between those in need of care living in private households and their family members, on the one hand, and the professional care services operating on the basis of the Long-Term Care Insurance Act, on the other hand. Care by ambulant care services is oriented towards principles of efficiency and standardization of care, which stands in opposition to the model of a flexible, socially embedded care adjusted to individual needs that is dominant among families. The disassociation of professional care work and social relationships also conflicts with the requirements of the person in need of care and their family members, who need socially embedded care based on trust, attention and recognition. These discrepancies between models with regard to a good quality of care lead to the uptake of the provision of professional care services turning out far lower than was to be expected as a consequence of the introduction of long-term care insurance.

Conclusion

With the introduction of the Long-Term Care Insurance Act (*Pflegeversicherungsgesetz*) in Germany in 1995/6, a new institutional framework was created for the organization of care in private households. However, the new option it created for elderly people in need of care and their families, to claim free basic coverage in the area of ambulant care by care services instead of or in addition to family care, has been comparatively little used. This contribution shows that the newly emerged possibilities have been used far less than could have been expected: the majority of those in need of care are still cared for exclusively by family members. In this chapter we discussed the question of the factors contributing to the explanation.

We argued that elderly persons in need of care often do not act as autonomous actors who choose between different offers on welfare markets. Instead, the decision is in many cases taken in a complex family context. On the basis of data from several representative surveys, we showed that orientation towards cultural values of moral responsibility and family solidarity offers an important foundation for explanation.

Based on our findings from guided interviews with caring family members of frail elderly people, we argue that there is a further cause of the comparatively low uptake of the provision offered by care services. There exists a mismatch between those in need of care and their families on the one hand, and professional providers on the other hand, with regard to attitudes to what should be understood as 'good' care.

This mismatch is especially exacerbated by the fact that professional care services are bound by the Long-Term Care Insurance Act to deliver care on the basis of principles of competitiveness, economic efficiency and Taylorization of workload. Care recipients and their family members often see good care as guaranteed only if the care is embedded in a trusting social relationship, and for this reason they sometimes turn down care by care services. Financial considerations appear to be of only secondary importance in the decision for care to be carried out exclusively by family members. This mismatch between the expectations of care households and the type of care offered by professional services contributes to the fact that care households continue in many cases not to involve ambulant care services in care, even though family members involved in care are often heavily overburdened and run the risk of social isolation.

It can be assumed that, particularly in those countries which have a relatively strong tradition in family care, people have difficulties in accepting care services in elder care which are aimed at supporting them to lead an autonomous life. Whereas in Nordic countries like Denmark and Finland, the proportion of people who prefer a formal solution is relatively high (Denmark: 75.4 per cent, Finland 67 per cent), the proportion of those who would decide in favour of a formal solution is much lower in countries like Germany, even though formal care is to a substantial degree publicly paid (West Germany 31.5 per cent, East Germany 37 per cent), Great Britain (38 per cent) and particularly also in Spain (13.5 per cent). In these countries, the great majority of people prefer informal family-based forms of care (see table 1).

Change could be promoted if the importance of trust and a good personal relationship between caregiver and care receiver were regarded in the way in which care is provided by long-term care agencies. However, it seems that marketization in part leads to the opposite type of care organization.

Table 1

Attitudes towards elder care in selected European countries Q.36. – Let's suppose you had an elderly father or mother who lived alone. What do you think would be the best thing to do if this parent could no longer manage to live on his/her own? (One answer only) (Accounts in percentages)

		Denmark	Germany/ West	Germany/ East	Spain	Great Britain	Finland
1	Myself or one of my brothers or sisters should invite my father or mother to live with one of us	8.9	39.4	32.7	66.9	30.2	12.1
2	I or one of my brothers or sisters should move in with my father or mother	1.1	5.7	3.5	6.4	4.3	3.7
3	One should move closer to the other	9.0	12.3	15.0	3.1	12.9	6.9
4	My father or mother should move into an old people's home or a nursing home	32.2	9.6	11.4	4.6	13.5	15.6
5	My father or mother should stay at home, and receive visits there, as well as appropriate health care and services	43.2	21.9	25.6	8.9	24.4	51.6
6	It depends (Spontaneous)	4.1	9.1	8.4	6.4	10.4	7.6
	No opinion	1.5	2.1	3.5	3.7	4.2	2.5
	Total	100	100	100	100	100	100

Source: INRA (Europe) Eurobarometer 50.1 – Autumn 1998; after Pfau-Effinger et al. (2009: 232).

Notes

1. In detail, the manner in which contributions are raised and claims for the provision of long-term care insurance are made is regulated as follows: everyone in gainful employment pays contributions to the long-term care insurance fund. Everyone who is certified as being in need of care on the basis of a health examination by the supervisory authority (*Medizinischer Dienst der Krankenkassen* (MDK)) is entitled to payments for necessary care from the long-term care insurance fund. Those in need of care may now choose between care by employees of a care service (benefits in kind), care by family members (or friends/acquaintances) (cash benefits), and a combination of the two.
2. In this study, 63 care arrangements were studied, and it was attempted to include all central figures of the care arrangement. Besides the person in need of care, the principal carer and, where relevant, professional carers were also interviewed. In addition to the question of the care relationship between the person in need of care and the carer, the organization of the care, the importance of the informal network and questions about experiences of professional care were also central to the interview.
3. The research project 'On the impact of the long-term care insurance on care arrangements in private households in East and West Germany' was financed by the Ministry of Science of the Federal Republic of Thuringia, Germany. It was carried out at the Universities of Hamburg and Jena and was directed by Birgit Pfau-Effinger, Ursula Dallinger and Christoph Köhler.
4. Multiple answers were permitted (see Mager 2007).
5. However, the survey gives no more detailed information on the extent to which this aspect is important for the decision between family care and care by a care service.

References

Alber, J. and Schölkopf, M. (1999), *Seniorenpolitik: die soziale Lage älterer Menschen in Deutschland und Europa* [Seniors policy: the social situation of older people in Germany and Europe], Amsterdam: Fakultas.
Backhaus-Maul, H. and Olk, T. (1997), Vom Korporatismus zum Pluralismus? – Aktuelle Tendenzen im Verhältnis zwischen Staat und Wohlfahrtsverbänden [From corporatism to pluralism? Current trends in the relationship between government and charities], *Theorie und Praxis der sozialen Arbeit*, 48, 3: 25–32.
Becker, G. S. (1993), Nobel lecture: the economic way of looking at behavior, *Journal of Political Economy*, 101, 3: 385–409.
Bode, I. (2005), Einbettung und Kontingenz: Wohlfahrtsmärkte und ihre Effekte im Spiegel der neueren Wirtschaftssoziologie [Embedding and contingency: welfare markets and their effects as reflected in recent economic sociology], *Zeitschrift für Soziologie*, 34, 4: 250–69.
Clarke, J. (2006), Consumer, clients or citizens? Politics, policy and practice in the reform of social care, *European Societies*, 8, 3: 423–42.
Deutscher Bundestag (2007), *Gesetzentwurf der Bundesregierung: Entwurf eines Gesetzes zur strukturellen Weiterentwicklung der Pflegeversicherung (Pflege-Weiterentwicklungsgesetz)* [Draft law of the Federal Government: Draft for further structural enhancements of the long-term care insurance], Drucksache: 16/7439, Berlin.
Deutscher Bundestag (2008), *Vierter Bericht über die Entwicklung der Pflegeversicherung* [Fourth report on the development of long-term care insurance], Drucksache: 16/7772, Berlin.

Dienel, C. (2007), Die Betreuung älterer Familienmitglieder im europäischen Vergleich – Perspektiven einer europäischen Politik für familiale Pflege [The care of elderly family members in a European comparison – perspectives of a European policy for family care], *Berliner Journal für Soziologie*, 17, 1: 281–300.

Eichler, M. (2005), Pflegeversicherung als Genderpolitik – Auswirkungen in Ost-und Westdeutschland: Forschungsbericht für das Teilprojekt 2 innerhalb des Forschungsprogramms 'Gender-Politiken' im Rahmen des HWP-Programms des Thüringer Wissenschaftsministeriums [Care insurance policy as a gender policy – effects in eastern and western Germany], *Jenaer Beiträge zur Soziologie*, 17.

Esping-Andersen, G. (1990), *The Three Worlds of Welfare Capitalism*, Cambridge: Polity Press.

Esping-Andersen, G. (1999), *The Social Foundations of Postindustrial Economies*, Oxford: Oxford University Press.

Fthenakis, W. E. and Textor, M. R. (1998), *Qualität von Kinderbetreuung: deutsche und internationale Perspektiven* [Quality of childcare: German and international perspectives], Freiburg: Lambertus.

Heusinger, J. and Klünder, M. (2005), *'Ich lass mir nicht die Butter vom Brot nehmen!' Aushandlungsprozesse in häuslichen Pflegearrangements* [Negotiation processes in domestic care arrangements], Frankfurt am Main: Mabuse-Verlag.

Knijn, T. (2000), Marketization and the struggling logics of (home) care in the Netherlands. In M. H. Meyer (ed.), *Care Work, Gender, Labor and the Welfare State*, London and New York: Routledge.

Lewis, J. (1992), Gender and the development of welfare regimes, *Journal of European Social Policy*, 2, 3: 73–91.

Lundsgaard, J. (2006), Choice and long-term care in OECD countries: care outcomes, employment and fiscal sustainability, *European Societies*, 8, 3: 361–83.

Mager, H.-C. (2007), Wenn Angehörige die Pflege übernehmen: Von Kosten und Nutzen intrafamiliärer Pflegevereinbarungen [When relatives care: the costs and benefits of intra-family care arrangements], *Forschung Frankfurt: Forschung aktuell*: 2. Available at: www.forschung-frankfurt.uni-frankfurt.de/dok/2007/2007-02/71-74_Pflege.pdf (accessed September 2008).

Mager, H.-C. and Eisen, R. (2002), Noch ist häusliche Pflege Familiensache. Die Pflegeversicherung und ihre Folgen [Domestic care is still a family affair. The long-term care insurance and its consequences], Forschung Frankfurt: *Forschung Intensiv*: 1–2. Available at: www.forschung-frankfurt.uni-frankfurt.de/dok/2002/2002-1u2/Pflegeversicherung_15-21.pdf (accessed December 2008).

Mayring, P. (1997), *Qualitative Inhaltsanalyse: Grundlagen und Techniken* [Qualitative content analysis: fundamentals and techniques], Weinheim: Dt.: Studien-Verlag.

Mischke, C. and Meyer, M. (2008), *'Am Ende habe ich gewusst, was ich am Anfang gerne gewusst hätte' Beratung Pflegender Angehöriger – Pflegeberatungsbedarfe im Verlauf von 'Pflegendenkarrieren' aus der Perspektive Pflegender Angehöriger, Projektabschlussbericht* [The need for care in the perspective of caring relatives. Research report], Saarbrücken: Hochschule für Technik und Wirtschaft des Saarlandes.

Motel-Klingebiel, A. (2002), *Lebensqualität und Alter. Generationenbeziehungen und öffentliche Servicesysteme im sozialen Wandel* [Quality of life and age. Intergenerational relations and public services under conditions of social change], Opladen: Leske+Budrich.

Ostner, I. (1998), The politics of care policies in Germany. In J. Lewis (ed.), *Gender, Social Care and Welfare State Restructuring in Europe*, Aldershot: Ashgate, pp. 111–37.

Pabst, S. (1999), Mehr Arbeitsplätze für Geringqualifizierte nach Einführung der Pflegeversicherung? Beschäftigungswirkungen des SGB XI im ambulanten Bereich [More jobs for low-skilled workers after the introduction of the long-term care insurance legislation?], *WSI-Mitteilungen*, 4: 234–40.

Pavolini, E. and Ranci, C. (2008), Restructuring the welfare state: reforms in long-term care in Western European countries, *Journal of European Social Policy*, 18, 3: 246–59.

Pfau-Effinger, B. (2004), *Development of Culture, Welfare States and Women's Employment in Europe*, Aldershot: Ashgate.

Pfau-Effinger, B., Eichler, M. and Och, R. (2007), Ökonomisierung, Pflegepolitik und Strukturen der Pflege älterer Menschen [Strengthening of economic principles, policies towards long-term care and care structures]. In A. Evers and R. Heinze (eds), *Sozialpolitik: Ökonomisierung und Entgrenzung*, Wiesbaden: VS-Verlag für Sozialwissenschaften, pp. 83–98.

Pfau-Effinger, B., Eichler, M. and Och, R. (2008), Ökonomisierung und die widersprüchlichen Dynamiken im gesellschaftlichen Arrangement der Altenpflege [Economization and the contradictory dynamics in elderly care arrangements]. In K.-S. Rehberg (ed.), *Die Natur der Gesellschaft. Verhandlungen des 33. Kongresses der Deutschen Gesellschaft für Soziologie in Kassel 2006*, Frankfurt am Main, New York: Campus, pp. 2665–77.

Pfau-Effinger, B., Jensen, P. H. and Flaquer, L. (2009), A comparative perspective on formal and informal work. In B. Pfau-Effinger, L. Flaquer and P. Jensen (eds), *Formal and Informal Work in Europe: The Hidden Work Regime*, New York: Routledge, pp. 193–214.

Rostgaard, T. (2006), Constructing the care consumer – free choice of home care for the elderly in Denmark, *European Societies*, 8, 3: 443–63.

Runde, P., Giese, R. and Stierle, C. (2003), *Bericht Einstellungen und Verhalten zur häuslichen Pflege und zur Pflegeversicherung unter den Bedingungen gesellschaftlichen Wandels: Analysen und Empfehlungen auf der Basis von repräsentativen Befragungen bei AOK-Leistungsempfängern der Pflegeversicherung* [Report on attitudes and practices of home care and care insurance under conditions of social change on the basis of a representative survey], Hamburg: Arbeitsstelle Rehabilitations-und Präventionsforschung.

Schmidt, R. (2002), Die neue Pflegelandschaft. Erste Konturen und Steuerungsprobleme [The new care landscape. First outline and governance problems]. In C. Tesch-Römer (ed.), *Gerontologie und Sozialpolitik* [Gerontology and social policy], Stuttgart, Berlin and Köln: Kohlhammer, pp. 137–62.

Schmidt, R. and Klie, T. (1998), Neupositionierung Sozialer Arbeit mit alten Menschen? Wirkungen von Wettbewerbselementen und neuen Steuerungsmodellen auf die Gestalt einer Profession [Repositioning of social work with the elderly? The impact of competition and new public management on a profession], *Zeitschrift für Gerontologie und Geriatrie*, 31, 5: 304–12.

Schneekloth, U. (2005a), *Leben mit Hilfe und Pflege zu Hause – Möglichkeiten und Grenzen –Zentrale Ergebnisse des Forschungsprojekts MuG III im Überblick* [Living with help and care at home – possibilities and limitations]. Paper presented at the final conference of a research consortium, 16 June, Berlin.

Schneekloth, U. (2005b), Entwicklungstrends beim Hilfe-und Pflegebedarf in Privathaushalten – Ergebnisse der Infratest-Repräsentativerhebung [Tendencies of development in the requirement for help and care in private households – results of the Infratest representative study]. In U. Schneekloth and H.-W. Wahl (eds), *Möglichkeiten und Grenzen selbständiger Lebensführung in privaten Haushalten (MuG III)* [Possibilities and limits of independent living in private households], Berlin: Bundesministerium für Familie, Senioren, Frauen und Jugend, pp. 55–98.

Schulz-Nieswandt, F. (2002), Wettbewerb in der Altenpflege? [Competition in elder care?] In C. Tesch-Römer (ed.), *Gerontologie und Sozialpolitik* [Gerontology and social policy], Stuttgart, Berlin and Köln: Kohlhammer, pp. 163–74.

Schütte, W. (2007), Freiwillige Pflege: Angehörige und sozial Engagierte – Kritik des Pflegegeldes [Care provided by relatives and volunteers – criticism on cash benefits]. In G. Igl, G. Naegele and S. Hamdorf (eds), *Reform der Pflegeversicherung – Auswirkungen auf die Pflegebedürftigen und die Pflegpersonen* [Reform of the care insurance – consequences for those in need of care and for carers], Schriftenreihe Sozialrecht und Sozialpolitik in Europa, vol. 2, Münster: Lit Verlag, pp. 152–65.

Theobald, H., Burau, V. and Blank, R. H. (2007), Choice in home-based elder care in different European countries: conflicts and outcomes in combining different logics. Paper presented at the 5th ESPAnet conference, 20–22 September, Vienna.

Ungerson, C. (2005), Gender, labour markets and care work in five European funding regimes. In B. Pfau-Effinger and B. Geissler (eds), *Care and Social Integration in European Societies*, Bristol: Policy Press, pp. 49–71.

Vabo, M. (2006), Caring for people or caring for proxy consumers? *European Societies*, 8, 3: 403–22.

7
A Comparative Discussion of the Gendered Implications of Cash-for-Care Schemes: Markets, Independence and Social Citizenship in Crisis?

Kirstein Rummery

Introduction

Political, social, economic and demographic changes in developed welfare states have led to concerns about rising demand for services, particularly support services for older and disabled people (Pierson 2001). On the 'demand' side, increased longevity, reduced morbidity and political pressure from citizens and service users has led to a growing realization among policy-makers and practitioners that present service levels, particularly in health and social care services, are inadequately funded and failing to respond effectively and efficiently to people's needs (Taylor-Gooby 2005). On the 'supply' side, falling birth rates and changes in family structures, as well as neo-liberal changes to welfare provision which have stressed the importance of activation policies (for example, welfare-to-work programmes for women, lone parents, disabled people and the long-term unemployed), and changing relations and expectations within families and communities have meant that there are falling numbers of 'unpaid' and family carers available and there have been substantial changes to the 'welfare mix' of contributions from the family, the state, the market and the third sector (Evers *et al.* 1994).

There have been long-standing concerns within developed welfare states about to how to manage welfare and care policies in a way which caps the rising demand for resources, leading to a shifting of responsibilities across public sectors (for example, from health to social care, and from national to localized provision), and across sectors (for example, from state to private or third sector provision, or from state to family [or, indeed, family to state]). At the same time a variety of international, national and local political, social and economic factors have led to changes in the governance of welfare, including increasing commodification of services and deprofessionalization of practitioners (Newman 2005). Rising demand for support and services has also come not just from demographic changes but also from increasingly politicized 'user' movements (such as disability rights organizations in the UK and the Netherlands, and older people's organizations in the USA) which have rejected both family and informal care as exploitative (for both carers and cared-for) and state care as increasingly fragmented, unresponsive and dehumanizing – indeed, rejecting the rhetoric of 'care' altogether and demanding social rights, empowerment and control over the type and level of support received instead (Morris 2004). Increasing regulation of services in response to 'consumer' demand has only partially succeeded in responding effectively to these changes: new models of service delivery are being actively sought in response to these complex political, social and economic changes (Ungerson and Yeandle 2007).

These pressures have led to the development of 'cash-for-care' schemes across a range of developed welfare states. Although these vary considerably in their intentions, their scope and the way they function, they are essentially mechanisms whereby a disabled or older person receives a cash benefit in order to purchase help or services themselves, in lieu of receiving services or support directly. They can be seen as a way of 'commodifying' care (Ungerson 1997), and several different models have emerged: tightly controlled personal care budgets allowing direct employment of formal care workers; care allowances paid directly to disabled and older people but not directly governed; income maintenance approaches (whereby allowances are paid directly to carers to acknowledge or compensate for the loss of earned income, usually only available to low-income carers); and directly paying informal carers to replace publicly funded formal care. In some forms, particularly those paid directly to disabled and older people, their popularity is well documented: they have been hailed as an important victory for social rights by campaigners in the UK, because of the way in which they have allowed disabled and older people to exert choice and control over the type of assistance and support they receive (Rummery 2006), and the way in which they have enabled disabled people to combine different types of support (health and social care, formal and informal) in ways which have led to greater independence and social participation, without the 'burden of gratitude' experienced by people receiving informal care from family members or voluntary or paid workers not directly employed by the disabled or older person themselves (Galvin 2004).

A gendered analysis of care work and its relationship to women's oppression has been the subject of feminist attention since Mary Wollstonecraft articulated the dilemma of whether to pursue equality by feminizing the public, male sphere or by masculinizing the private, female sphere (Pateman 1988; Lister 2003). Much attention has been paid to citizenship and care policies, with commentators pointing out that welfare states often accord women a second-class citizenship because of their involvement in caring for both children and disabled and older adults, while at the same time relying on care work being carried out in a way which does not undermine the working of a capitalist economy (Fraser 1994). A long-running debate within feminist social policy has been taking place: writers such as Dalley (1988) and others on the one hand, who, building on the understanding of the way in which care work is gendered and leads to gender-based oppression have pointed out that 'policy is personal' (Ungerson 1987), have argued for greater state involvement in the provision of care and support for disabled and older people. Morris (2004) and others, on the other hand, building on the understanding of the way in which lack of control over the care and support they receive leads to disabled people's oppression, point out that disabled (and older) women receiving care are subject to patriarchal *and* 'ablist' oppression. What has been missing from that debate is an understanding of the complex nature of women's lives and the way in which 'care' and support are often reciprocal, and that the quest for independence and control over their lives is one shared by carers and disabled and older people alike (Lloyd 2000; Rummery 2007).

Cash-for-care policies have not been traditionally seen as examples of gender mainstreaming or of feminist social policy, but, like any other policy development, they have 'deep normative cores' (Sabatier 1999) that dictate both why and how the policies have been developed and implemented, and these 'deep normative cores' have been implicitly gendered, resting on sometimes unarticulated but nonetheless powerful normative assumptions about the acceptable role and value of care work as 'feminized' (and hence legitimately undervalued in market terms) and 'private' (and hence legitimately underpoliced by the state) (Lewis 2002). This has the result that both the aims and outcomes of the policies have gendered impacts in both covert and overt ways, but because the policies themselves have not been overtly articulated as gendered these have been underexplored. It is the purpose of this chapter to address that gap. The next section will give a brief overview of cash-for-care policy developments in six developed welfare states, before going on to discuss: how 'gender-aware' or 'gender-blind' the development of cash-for-care policies has been; the governance issues raised, the development and implementation of cash-for-care policies, and the gendered implications of these; the gendered impact of such policies on the division of paid and unpaid work, citizenship and social participation; the impact such policies have, or are likely to have, on different groups of women across the life course and across different social and economic groups; and how such policies can contribute to the well-being and/or detriment of different groups of women within different social, political and economic contexts. The chapter will conclude with some reflections on how the successful commodification/marketization of independence for disabled people can be reconciled with the concerns about gender equity in social citizenship.

Examples of Cash-for-Care Policies

There are many ways of comparatively classifying welfare regimes, but the most commonly used are those developed from Esping-Andersen's *Three Worlds of Welfare* thesis (Esping-Andersen 1990), which divided welfare states into 'liberal' (in which means-tested assistance and modest universal or insurance transfers take place, and the free market is seen as the best way for distributing resources, with the state supporting it, such as the UK and the USA), 'conservative' (in which state-led social policy development reflected invested interests that are neither purely social democratic nor market-driven,

Table 1

Cash-for-care schemes by welfare typology

Country	Welfare typology	People over 65 receiving formal help at home (%)[*]
UK	Liberal[1] informal care[2]	5.5
Netherlands	Conservative[1] informal care[2]	12.0
Italy	Conservative[1] family care[2]	2.8
France	Conservative[1] formal care[2]	6.1
Austria	Conservative[1] public/private care	24.0
USA	Liberal[1]	16.0

*From Casey et al. (2003). [1]Esping Andersen (1990). [2]Bettio and Plantenga (2004).

such as the Netherlands, Italy, France and Austria), and 'universal' (where a commitment to universalism and decommodification involves the state working outside the market, such as the Nordic welfare states). Bettio and Plantenga (2004) have extended and nuanced this analysis with respect to European care regimes and found five typologies: countries that rely on the family for all care (Italy, Greece, Spain); countries that rely on informal care (but more so for childcare than adult care) (UK, Netherlands); countries with state-facilitated private care (Austria, Germany); countries with highly developed formal care (France); and those with moderate to high levels of formal care (Denmark, Finland, Sweden) (see table 1).

It is perhaps worth noting at this point that no case study examples of cash-for-care schemes have been included from either Esping-Andersen's 'universal' nor Bettio and Plantenga's 'moderate/high informal care' regimes, as schemes in these countries have either been relatively underdeveloped, or have not followed the marketized route of enabling direct employment of carers.

United Kingdom

In the United Kingdom a system of direct payments was introduced in 1996 which replaced previous ad hoc schemes. Disabled and older people are now able to apply for payments in lieu of directly provided services (the level of which are set according to a needs assessment) and these payments are usually used to directly employ formal care workers, or purchase care from not-for-profit care agencies. It is not possible to directly pay family members, as, unlike other schemes, the system is intended to replace formal rather than informal care and support, and there is relatively low take-up among older people. A regulatory system is in place, although there is little formal employment protection for directly employed workers, and lack of formal assistance in recruitment of care workers is a problem for both users and employees. It is implemented locally, with the result that there is considerable regional variation in criteria, eligibility and access, although policy developments are in place to support more systematic take-up and to enable users to purchase a wider range of services (at present the scheme is limited to 'social' care) (Rummery 2006).

The Netherlands

The Netherlands has seen the introduction in 1991 of a personal care allowance scheme that was extended in 1995 to become part of the national long-term care insurance scheme (Pijl and Ramakers 2007), allowing recipients to choose to receive direct payments in lieu of directly provided services. This scheme is relatively strictly regulated, providing a degree of protection for directly employed care workers and making it impossible to pay workers directly on the 'black' or unregulated market. However, it can be used to purchase care from family members and thus enables recipients to combine formal and informal care arrangements flexibly. It is also relatively generously funded, leading to political concerns about rising demand, although, in common with other cash-for-care schemes it is still cheaper than directly providing state-funded services (Weekers and Pijl 1998).

Italy

Italy has historically seen very little development of formal residential or community-based care services, explained in part by very decentralized state provision of services generally (leading to substantial regional variations), and a reliance on family and informal care, accompanied by a reluctance to develop formal, central state-driven responses to the rising demand for long-term care and support (Pavolini and Ranci 2006). The *Indennità di accompagnamento* is a non-means-tested benefit available to disabled and older people who are certified as 'dependent'. It is not tempered according to need, and no restrictions are placed upon its use. This comparative lack of regulation means that it is most often used to employ care workers, often on the black (unregulated) labour market (Ranci 2007; Gori and Da Roit 2007). Local means-tested care allowances, which are subject to local variations in terms of eligibility and access, are also available, and are also used primarily to purchase care from individual workers and family members, reinforcing gendered divisions of labour – or sometimes as a supplement to the family income and not paid out directly for care (Gori and Da Roit 2007).

France

France is usually viewed as a 'familialist' welfare state, with insurance-based health and social care payments coupled with a strong ethos of family-based care (Martin and Le Bihan 2007). In 1997 the *Prestation Spécifique Dépendance* (PSD) was introduced, which was replaced in 2002 by the *Allocation Personnalisée à l'Autonomie* (APA). This is a payment made directly to older people (which can be supplemented by other means-tested benefits) which enables them to purchase their own care directly, either from a professional or a relative (but not from a spouse). It is most commonly used to purchase services from formal, not-for-profit social care organizations, rather than directly employing individuals. It has been argued that this formalized element to the payment is an important part of France's strategy of protecting the employment rights of care workers, as well as reinforcing gendered divisions of low-paid formal and informal labour (Martin 2000). The more formalized APA system has led to more employment protection for professional carers (Bresse 2004), but it has not altered the gendered division of formal and informal care (Martin 2000).

Austria

Austria has traditionally been viewed as a strong social democratic state with an emphasis on a gendered division of labour and the 'male breadwinner' model of welfare provision, resulting in low levels of provision of formal care services (Bettio and Plantenga 2004). In 1993 the long-term care allowance (*Pflegegeld*) system was introduced, a tax-financed, non-means-tested benefit paid directly to the disabled or older person (Oesterle 2001). It is generally used to purchase care from either organizations or individuals, or to reimburse family members (Hammer and Oesterle 2003). It has tended to be used to fund informal care or migrant/'grey' labour market workers (often from neighbouring accession states), reinforcing traditions of low-paid workers (often women) with very little employment protection, while also reinforcing gendered divisions of labour within the familial sphere (Oesterle 2001; Kreimer and Schiffbaenker 2005).

The USA

A high degree of policy decentralization has led to considerable federal-level variation in American social care provision. Since 1981 Medicaid programmes in the USA have been allowed a greater discretion in providing services and support for older and disabled people, leading to a proliferation of 'consumer-choice' programmes allowing people to hire their own care workers directly, particularly through schemes such as the Cash and Counseling Demonstration pilots in Arkansas, Florida and New Jersey (Mahoney *et al.* 2000). These schemes usually allow disabled and older people to employ directly workers with whom they have an ongoing relationship (through kinship or long-term care relationships), and have proved popular and successful, with the result that such 'private market solutions' are becoming part of mainstream social care policy (Keigher 2007).

Gendered Policy Outcomes

Gender mainstreaming, broadly conceived, is the process by which gender equality becomes part of public policy strategy (Daly 2005). Despite the fact that, as Lewis points out, the question of who undertakes or pays for care is crucial in addressing women's oppression (Lewis 2006), developments towards gender mainstreaming social policies in care have focused more extensively on the issue of activation and childcare policies than on care and support for disabled and older people. It is clear, in looking across the different types of cash-for-care developments described above, that several normative cores or themes emerge, but none of them appears to be about addressing gender inequalities. Indeed, as will be seen below, some of the consequences of such policies will be to reinforce gender inequalities.

On the one hand, cash-for-care appears, in some cases, to be attempting to address neo-liberal concerns with reducing the role of the state in providing formal support (often accompanied by concerns about suppressing costs, particularly in cases where the policy is explicitly designed to support moves away from costly residential support, such as in the UK and the Netherlands). Certainly, advocates of state feminism would point out that when the state aims to reduce its role it usually expects the family to step in (Stetson and Mazur 1995) – and this will, overwhelmingly (but not exclusively) mean reinforcing gender inequalities through a reliance on family care. On the other hand, cash-for-care schemes can also be shown to be responding to demands from users for more responsive care and support, and more control over that care and support (the political campaigns from user groups in the UK, the Netherlands and the USA are evidence of this) (Donnellan 2001). While not overtly or exclusively about tackling gender-related oppression, part of that political argument has been about the exploitative nature of informal care for both carers and cared-for, as it reinforces both dependency and powerlessness for both parties (Morris 2004).

The other political argument that has had an overtly gendered dimension in cash-for-care scheme development has been around campaigns to recognize and recompense women's informal care work as part of a citizenship agenda (Lister 2002) – working towards carer-parity in welfare regimes (Fraser 1994). In the cases where cash-for-care is about replacing, or commodifying, *informal* care (such as Italy and Austria), it would appear that twin aims can be discerned that do show an awareness of gender-based inequality: first, by freeing up 'unpaid' carers to participate in the labour market, and second, by recompensing previously 'unpaid' carers for their care work. In the case where cash-for-care development was driven by a desire to protect the employment rights and status of formal care workers (France), given that these are overwhelmingly women, it could also be argued that this was a policy objective intended to address gender inequalities.

However, there is arguably a limit to how far an analysis of these policy developments can show them to be 'gender mainstreaming'. At best, an awareness of the gendered dimensions of care work can be said to have informed policy development: that is not the same as asserting that these policy developments were aiming to address gender inequalities. Other, more powerful, overarching policy drivers can be argued to be in play: specifically, the neo-liberal drive to reduce state involvement and expenditure on social care and, correspondingly, all the schemes under scrutiny can be shown to be justifying their existence on cost–benefit terms, with various mechanisms for cost containment (such as shifting overhead and employment costs, and the associated risks, on to users) being an important part of their *raison d'être*. Other, also more powerful, overarching policy drivers can be seen in the consumerist response to political pressure from users to promote autonomy, independence and user-controlled support. Neither of these policy drivers is mainstreaming gender issues; however, this does not mean that they do not have overtly gendered outcomes, as will be seen below.

Governance and Cash-for-Care Schemes

Two issues pertinent to the governance of cash-for-care schemes emerge from an analysis of the six schemes under discussion. First, there is the issue of national versus regional/local governance. Where schemes have been developed which allow for a degree of localized discretion in their implementation (e.g. the UK, the USA and, to a certain degree, Italy) there is considerable scope for inequalities and inequities inherent in the system to have a gendered impact (for example, in the different types of employment protection available to workers, and the differential impact commodifying care can have on family relationships).

Second, there is the issue of the governance of the schemes themselves: how they are operated, how users are made to account for the ways in which they spend money, and the level of policing and surveillance which that gives the state over individuals' lives. Some schemes (e.g. the UK, the Netherlands, France) are highly regulated, which, one the one hand, offers a degree of protection both to potentially vulnerable users and workers (and, particularly in the case of France, offers valuable employment protection to potentially exploited groups of care workers who are overwhelmingly women), but which, on the other hand, also gives the state a considerable degree of power to scrutinize and police intimate caring relationships, and limits the degree to which these relationships can be user-controlled or reflect complex, reciprocal obligations. Other schemes (for example, Austria and Italy) are explicitly and deliberately unregulated, allowing on the one hand a high degree of personal flexibility and control on the part of users and carers (reducing the state's role in policing care and regulating women's lives), but on the other hand sustaining an unregulated and unprotected employment market that has the potential to be exploitative to vulnerable groups of workers (overwhelmingly, but not exclusively, women), while at the same time reinforcing gendered divisions of labour that are potentially aggravating structural social and economic inequalities.

Gendered Divisions of Work

Given the considerable variations in political, social and economic aims, and governance arrangements, of the schemes under scrutiny, a remarkable consistency across all of them is that they have not made any significant impact on the gendered division of labour. Care work, whether paid or unpaid, is still overwhelmingly the responsibility of women in all six schemes. Perhaps because of the overarching policy objective of cost containment, in all schemes the actual value of payments to users has been deliberately set low (even in the comparatively expensive Netherlands scheme), which has had the result of reinforcing gendered inequalities: if routed as 'wages' to previously unpaid carers, they have the result of 'trapping' women into gendered expectations of delivering care while at the same time not adequately compensating them for the value of that care; if routed as actual wages to formal carers, they still have the result of 'trapping' women into underpaid and under-regulated employment, with poor prospects for formalized skills and training development or employment protection.

Divergent policy goals have led to differential policy outcomes regarding the gendered division of labour. Where cash-for-care schemes have incorporated a specific element designed to formalize and protect the status of employed carers (for example, through routing payments to recognized care agencies, such as in France and the Netherlands, or through governance mechanisms designed to scrutinize the level and quality of the care received, such as in the UK and the USA), this is likely to have the effect of 'polarizing' the care market (Ungerson and Yeandle 2007) – creating ever-increasing gaps between paid workers with structured career paths working in the non-profit and statutory sectors, and family or casual labour carers without the benefit of such regulation and protection. It is likely, as in other traditionally feminized caring professions that have become regulated and professionalized (such as education and nursing) that men will be attracted into the former, particularly into managerial roles, in much greater numbers than into the latter. This polarization of the care market is therefore likely to lead to greater gender inequalities in both the public, formal, regulated sphere and the private, informal, unregulated sphere of care provision.

Life-course and Social Divisions

In some respects, the introduction of a marketized, consumerist mechanism such as cash-for-care schemes into an area that was previously the domain of either the private, familial sphere or the public, statutory sphere is likely to create and exacerbate social divisions already apparent between different social groups. For example, the evidence on take-up of such schemes in the UK suggests that it is generally articulate, younger, well-educated disabled people who are disproportionately represented among those who choose to use them (Spandler 2004). Take-up among older people, ethnic minorities and learning disabled adults remains comparatively low. These findings echo concerns across other areas of welfare provision that consumerist-driven reforms will tend to favour those best placed to benefit from the market by exercising choice, voice and exit (6, 2003). In other words, the gulf between middle-class and poorer disabled and older people is likely to be made greater by the introduction of cash-for-care schemes, as is the gulf between middle-class and poorer carers, with the former being more able to exercise choice about the level and type of care work they undertake than the latter. As discussed above, cash-for-care schemes are also likely to lead to a widening gulf between carers working in regulated, professionalized and protected formal care employment and those working in private, unregulated employment, whether this be for a family member, a direct employer or through the grey/black labour market. They are likely to further disenfranchise low-skilled, poorly paid women in comparison to their wealthier, better-educated sisters and to widen social division within and across genders.

Furthermore, the impact of cash-for-care schemes on power relationships within the family sphere across the life course and across generations remains unexplored, but there are reasons to voice concern about several aspects. First, in low-income families where the use of the cash payment is fairly unregulated (for example in Italy) it is likely, based on what we already know about the distribution and use of money in low-income households, that gender differentials will emerge, with women more likely to use the payments to purchase care and men being more likely to use the payments as part of the general household income (Vogler and Pahl 1993), leading to a reinforcement of gendered power differences within families. Second, where cash-for-care schemes are used to route money to informal family carers, this can have the effect of creating or reinforcing dependency relationships both inter-generationally (for example, between learning disabled adult children and parent/carers; or between daughters/daughters-in-law and parents) and intra-generationally (for example, between spouses). Finally, the use of unregulated and unsupervised cash-for-care payments, both to pay family carers and directly employ unskilled care workers, has the result of commodifying intimate and sometimes unarticulated relationships and expectations, with the possibility of exploitation and abuse of vulnerable parties on both sides (Ungerson 2004). Money, after all, in a highly consumer-oriented capitalist society, is power, and the person controlling the money in a care relationship is in a position to be able to exert power and influence over the person who does not: and any relationship involving the exercise of power and control over another person is open to the possibility of the abuse of that power and control. Again, better-educated, better-skilled and better-paid women are likely to be in a better position to avoid the potential abuse and exploitation suffered by less-educated, lower-skilled and lower-paid women in these situations, leading to greater inequalities between different groups of women (and sometimes men).

Well-being and Citizenship

Notwithstanding the issues and concerns raised above, the evidence across all the schemes, particularly in comparative and qualitative studies (see, for example, Glendinning and Kemp 2006; Ungerson and Yeandle 2007), suggests that such schemes do appeal to both users and formal and informal carers, and it is worth exploring some of the gendered dimensions of why this is the case. First, cash-for-care schemes are a way of recognizing the complexity and reciprocity that characterize many caring relationships. One thing that both feminist and disability rights researchers and campaigners have pointed out is that people's identities within the social world are not easily divided into binary distinctions: public versus private, user versus carer, worker versus non-worker. It is possible – indeed, usual – for disabled and older people to be simultaneously employers (for example, of personal care workers), carers (for example, of spouses, children or grandchildren), workers (whether full- or part-time, paid or unpaid, voluntary or involuntary, or a combination of all of these) and to be exercising citizenship rights and duties in other complex ways (Lloyd 2000; Rummery 2007). The advantage of cash-for-care schemes over the alternatives (i.e. formal state provision or informal family provision of care and support) is that giving choice and control to disabled and older people enables them to purchase care and support that fits in with both statutory and informal networks, and enables them to carry out their own caring and other duties (Rummery 2006).

Second, cash-for-care schemes are a very effective way of filling in gaps between service provision that are not easily addressed by formal provision – for example, by enabling users to employ workers who cross the 'health/social' care divide, or by allowing users to purchase support for themselves in a caring role (e.g. as a parent) – which can have the result of ameliorating the effects of power dependencies within families. The effects of freeing people up (to be parents, spouses and children, rather than carers and/or cared-for) can have a significantly positive effect on the well-being and relationships of all concerned. Exercising choice and control is empowering not only for users but also for carers: being able to choose when and how to care and being able to choose *not* to care can reduce the disempowering effects of having to provide care because no other options are available. As women are still the primary carers in families, their concerns are with the well-being of all their families, and a policy development that has the effect of increasing the well-being of all members of the family is one to be welcomed.

Finally, if we move away from a neo-liberal economic analysis of cash-for-care schemes as being a way of trapping women into low-paid, unskilled care work, towards a more nuanced understanding of the *value* of care work and an 'ethic of care' (Sevenhuijsen 1998), both for carers and cared-for, we can conceivably argue that giving women the opportunity to engage in that work for payment, even if that payment is low, is possibly opening up citizenship opportunities in a way that is preferable to some of the alternatives available. For example, engaging in care work, particularly if freely chosen, is arguably less dangerous and exploitative to low-paid migrant workers than other black-market alternatives: any gendered analysis would have difficulty asserting that contributing to the well-being of disabled and older people is of less importance than contributing to the well-being of the purchasers of sexual services, for example.

Conclusions: Cash-for-Care Schemes, Empowerment and Choice

A gendered analysis of cash-for-care schemes therefore throws up some interesting challenges and contradictions. On the one hand, there are some very real concerns for gender equality heralded by the development and extension of these schemes. The overarching policy objective of cost-containment means both that the risks (such as covering for gaps in provision, and employing and managing care workers) are devolved to users and absorbed by them and their families, and that the level of payments has been set so low that carers employed by such schemes (whether they are agency workers, privately employed workers or previously unpaid family members) are having to work long hours for low pay with often little employment protection or direct scrutiny of their labour, and are therefore vulnerable to exploitation, abuse, and being trapped into low-paid work with little prospect of improving their skills or career development. The potential for social divisions (for example, between well-educated and poorly-skilled workers, and between well-supported and more vulnerable users) to be created and exacerbated by cash-for-care schemes is significant, as is the potential for the reinforcement of gendered divisions in labour. The governance of cash-for-care schemes also highlights potential problems, with issues of concern arising both from over-governance (the limitations placed on how money can be used, the opening up of women's lives to further state scrutiny and policing) and under-governance (the potential for exploitation and abuse, particularly of grey/black labour market workers and family members).

On the other hand, there are some very real potential gains in terms of gender equity, if not equality, in terms of well-being and citizenship that arise from cash-for-care schemes that cannot be ignored. These appear to derive mainly from the introduction of choice and control into relationships that may have previously been characterized by disempowering obligations, burdens of gratitude and inflexible formal services. Allowing disabled and older people to freely choose who supports them, how, and when enables them to exercise control in their lives, combine giving and receiving care and support in ways which free them to exercise their duties and choices as independent citizens. This can have a significant impact on their well-being and on their ability to work, care and contribute to the well-being of their families, communities and society as a whole. Correspondingly, allowing carers to freely choose whether to engage in paid and/or unpaid care (because cash-for-care schemes can work to either free unpaid carers to be engaged in other paid work, or, in cases where cash is routed to pay previously unpaid family members, to reimburse them and alleviate the constrictions caused by poverty) can free them from disempowering obligations, having a significant impact on their well-being and their ability to work, care and contribute to the well-being of their families, communities and society as a whole.

Of course, engaging in a gendered analysis of the policy impacts of cash-for-care schemes is problematic, because they are not explicitly gendered policy developments. However, as this analysis has shown, even gender-neutral or gender-blind policies can have significantly gendered outcomes (Rummery et al. 2007). The six cash-for-care schemes under scrutiny in this chapter appear to fall into three groups: schemes whereby some protection against the potential negative gender-effects of the policy is offered by the relatively high degree of formalization (France and the Netherlands); schemes whereby some degree of protection against abuse is offered by a degree of scrutiny and limits on paying family members, but the high degree of discretion and variability in operation offer the potential for some negative gendered impacts (the UK and the USA); and schemes whereby existing significant gender inequalities are likely to be exacerbated by the low levels of state governance (Austria and Italy). Interestingly, the most positive outcomes for disabled and older people would appear to be in the most formalized schemes

(France and the Netherlands), which would lead us to conclude that what is good for gender equality and equity is good for other groups of society too, and that a benign-but-powerful welfare state has an important role to play in protecting the citizenship rights of women, disabled people and older people.

However, as the pressures of rising demand, increased longevity and social and economic changes leading to higher labour market participation generally for women are global and affect developed welfare states of all political constituencies, it will be interesting to observe whether the type of commodification characterized by cash-for-care schemes will be adopted across different welfare regimes, and what the gendered impacts of those will be. It is clear that marketized solutions involving the commodification of care can offer gains in social citizenship for users *and* carers if the state is prepared to have a strong influence over the governance of such solutions while still enabling both groups to exercise choice and control: it is also clear that marketized solutions involving the commodification of care can offer potentially worrying effects on the social citizenship of users and carers if the market is left unchecked.

References

Bettio, F. and Plantenga, J. (2004), Comparing care regimes in Europe, *Feminist Economics*, 10, 1: 85–113.
Bresse, S. (2004), Le personnel des services d'aide à domicile en 1999 [Personnel of home help services in 1999], *Etudes et Resultants*, 297: 1–7.
Casey, B., Oxley, H., Whitehouse, E. *et al.* (2003), *Policies for an Ageing Society: Recent Measures and Areas for Further Reform*, Paris: OECD.
Dalley, G. (1988), *Ideologies of Caring: Rethinking Community and Collectivism*, Basingstoke: Macmillan.
Daly, M. (2005), Gender mainstreaming in theory and practice, *Social Politics*, 13, 3: 433–50.
Donnellan, C. (2001), *Disability Rights*, London: Independence.
Esping-Andersen, G. (1990), *The Three Worlds of Welfare Capitalism*, Cambridge: Polity Press.
Evers, A., Pijl, M. and Ungerson, C. (1994), *Payments for Care: A Comparative Overview*, Aldershot: Avebury.
Fraser, N. (1994), After the family wage: gender equity and the welfare state, *Political Theory*, 22, 4: 591–618.
Galvin, R. (2004), Challenging the need for gratitude: comparisons between paid and unpaid care for disabled people, *Journal of Sociology*, 40, 2: 137–55.
Glendinning, C. and Kemp, P. A. (eds) (2006), *Cash and Care: Policy Challenges in the Welfare State*, Bristol: Policy Press.
Gori, G. and Da Roit, B. (2007), The commodification of care – the Italian way. In C. Ungerson and S. Yeandle (eds), *Cash for Care in Developed Welfare States*, Basingstoke: Palgrave Macmillan, pp. 60–80.
Hammer, E. and Oesterle, A. (2003), Welfare state policy and informal long-term care giving in Austria: old gender divisions and new stratification processes among women, *Journal of Social Policy*, 32, 1: 37–53.
Keigher, S. (2007), Consumer direction in an ownership society: an emerging paradigm for home and community care in the United States. In C. Ungerson and S. Yeandle (eds), *Cash for Care in Developed Welfare States*, Basingstoke: Palgrave Macmillan, pp. 166–86.

Kreimer, M. and Schiffbaenker, H. (2005), The Austrian care arrangement and the role of informal care for social integration. In B. Pfau-Effinger and B. Geissler (eds), *Care and Social Integration in European Societies*, Bristol: Policy Press, pp. 173–95.

Lewis, J. (2002), Gender and welfare state change, *European Societies*, 4, 4: 331–57.

Lewis, J. (2006), Care and gender: have the arguments for recognising care work now been won? In C. Glendinning and P. Kemp (eds), *Cash and Care: Policy Challenges in the Welfare State*, Bristol: Policy Press, pp. 11–20.

Lister, R. (2002), The dilemmas of pendulum politics: balancing paid work, care and citizenship, *Economy and Society*, 31, 4: 520–34.

Lister, R. (2003), *Citizenship: Feminist Perspectives*, Basingstoke: Macmillan.

Lloyd, L. (2000), Caring about carers – only half the picture? *Critical Social Policy*, 20, 1: 136–50.

Mahoney, K. J., Simone, K. and Simon-Rusinowitz, L. (2000), Early lessons for the cash and counseling demonstration and evaluation, *Generations*, 24, 3: 41–6.

Martin, C. (2000), Atouts et limites de l'experimentation: l'exemple de la prestation dépendance [Strengths and limitations of experiment: the example of dependency benefit], *Revue Française des Affaires Sociales*, 1: 47–58.

Martin, C. and Le Bihan, B. (2007), Cash for care in the French welfare state: a skilful compromise? In C. Ungerson and S. Yeandle (eds), *Cash for Care in Developed Welfare States*, Basingstoke: Palgrave Macmillan, pp. 32–59.

Morris, J. (2004), Independent living and community care: a disempowering framework, *Disability and Society*, 19, 5: 427–42.

Newman, J. (ed.) (2005), *Remaking Governance: Peoples, Politics and the Public Sphere*, Bristol: Policy Press.

Oesterle, A. (2001), *Equity Choices and Long-term Care Policies in Europe: Allocating Resources and Burdens in Austria, Italy, the Netherlands and the United Kingdom*, Aldershot: Ashgate.

Pateman, C. (1988), *The Sexual Contract*, Cambridge: Polity Press.

Pavolini, E. and Ranci, C. (2006), New trends of elderly care policy in Western Europe: towards a social market of care services? Presented at the 16th ISA World Congress of Sociology, Durban.

Pierson, P. (2001), *New Politics of the Welfare State*, Oxford: Oxford University Press.

Pijl, M. and Ramakers, C. (2007), Contracting one's family members: the Dutch care allowance. In C. Ungerson and S. Yeandle (eds), *Cash for Care in Developed Welfare States*, Basingstoke: Palgrave Macmillan, pp. 81–103.

Ranci, C. (2007), Crisis and transformation of the Italian care model: beyond familism, the role of the market and public policies. Presented at ESPA-Net Annual Conference, Vienna.

Rummery, K. (2006), Disabled citizens and social exclusion: the role of direct payments, *Policy and Politics*, 34, 4: 633–50.

Rummery, K. (2007), Caring, citizenship and New Labour: dilemmas and contradictions for disabled and older women. In C. Annesley, F. Gains and K. Rummery (eds), *Women and New Labour: Engendering Politics and Policy?* Bristol: Policy Press, pp. 175–93.

Rummery, K., Gains, F. and Annesley, C. (2007), New Labour: towards an engendered politics and policy? In C. Annesley, F. Gains and K. Rummery (eds), *Women and New Labour: Engendering Politics and Policy?* Bristol: Policy Press, pp. 231–51.

Sabatier, P. (ed.) (1999), *Theories of the Policy Process*, New York: Westview Press.

Sevenhuijsen, S. (1998), *Citizenship and the Ethics of Care: Feminist Considerations on Justice, Morality and Politics*, London: Routledge.

6,P. (2003), Giving consumers of British public services more choice: what can be learned from recent history? *Journal of Social Policy*, 32, 2: 239–70.

Spandler, H. (2004), Friend or foe? Towards a critical assessment of direct payments, *Critical Social Policy*, 24, 2: 187–209.

Stetson, D. M. and Mazur, A. (eds) (1995), *Comparative State Feminism*, London: Sage.

Taylor-Gooby, P. (2005), *Welfare Reform and the Management of Societal Change*, Brussels: DG Research, European Commission.

Ungerson, C. (1987), *Policy is Personal: Sex, Gender and Informal Care*, London: Routledge.

Ungerson, C. (1997), Social politics and the commodification of care, *Social Politics*, 4, 3: 362–81.

Ungerson, C. (2004), Whose empowerment and independence? A cross-national perspective on 'cash-for-care' schemes, *Ageing and Society*, 24, 2: 189–212.

Ungerson, C. and Yeandle, S. (eds) (2007), *Cash for Care in Developed Welfare States*, Basingstoke: Palgrave Macmillan.

Vogler, C. and Pahl, J. (1993), Social and economic change and the organisation of money within marriage, *Work, Employment and Society*, 7, 1: 71–95.

Weekers, S. and Pijl, M. (1998), *Home Care and Care Allowances in the European Union*, Utrecht: NIZW.

8
Challenging Solidarity? An Analysis of Exit Options in Social Policies

Menno Fenger

Introduction

The introduction of new public management in modern welfare states has not only led to significant changes in the way social services are delivered by focusing on efficiency and performance. In addition, new public management has also contributed to the quality of services and the orientation on the wants and needs of clients and consumers (see Pollitt 2003). The chapters in this book deal with the evolution of free choice in modern welfare states. In this chapter, I focus on a specific element of free choice: the introduction of exit options in social policies. Exit options are the options that are available to individuals to cancel, or partly cancel, their participation in previously mandatory institutions of social policy. When the people that use exit options are a representative sample of society, exit options are hardly worth a discussion of their own. It is to be expected that the group of people that decides to exit health insurances, unemployment insurances or other welfare institutions, is the group of people with relatively low risks, that expect to be 'better off' by not participating. For this reason, exit options might form an important challenge for solidarity in modern welfare states that have not been given substantial empirical and theoretical attention in the literature on welfare states. Rosanvallon (2000) is a well known and inspiring exception to this, although he focuses on the information that individuals have on their own risks, instead of on the institutional options.

   To study the impact of exit options on the occurrence of adverse selection, this chapter analyses the introduction of exit options in four European countries: the Netherlands, Spain, Sweden and the UK. Although all welfare state classifications are somewhat arbitrary, I start from the premise that European welfare states might be classified into four different types. The Netherlands serves as an example of the continental welfare states, the UK as an illustration for the Anglo-Saxon welfare states, Sweden for the Scandinavian type and Spain as an example of the southern European welfare states. Of course, both the typology and the question to what extent countries fit into the ideal types are the subject of fierce scientific debate. However, this selection of countries enables a broad overview of the prevalence and impact of exit options in European welfare states. Three domains of the welfare states are selected: health insurances, unemployment schemes, and pension schemes.

The chapter focuses on three questions. The first is to what extent exit options have been introduced in the domains of health insurances, unemployment schemes and pension schemes in the four countries. This question is answered by an analysis of the legal framework and other official documents. Second, the chapter focuses on the extent to which these exit options actually are used by people. To answer this question, statistical material and evaluations have been studied. The final question is to what extent adverse selection has occurred. This requires a more in-depth comparison of the characteristics of the people that have decided to use the exit options and the remaining participants. By answering these three questions, the chapter reflects on the consequences of opting out for solidarity in European welfare states.

The next section discusses the relation between free choice and exit options. Then I focus on the issue of adverse selection and its relation to solidarity. Then the extent to which exit options have been introduced and their practical consequences are discussed for the domains of health policies, unemployment policies and pension schemes in each of the four countries. Finally, I draw conclusions on the consequences of exit options for adverse selection, and discuss the theoretical and practical implications of these findings.

Free Choice and Opting Out

The evolution of modern welfare states is characterized by a gradual extension of the coverage of insurances. For instance, health insurances, unemployment insurances and pensions started within small, professional circles like guilds. It appeared that extension of the coverage and diversification of the participants significantly increased the viability of these welfare state institutions. This has led to universal or near-universal coverage for most of the key institutions of modern welfare states.

The implementation of the ideas of new public management in social policies has introduced elements of free choice in social security schemes in several countries (see also Greener 2008). More choice has then often been linked with a wish to have increased competition between welfare providers, for instance through the use of per-user funding, vouchers and tax credits. Moreover, the introduction of free choice might also enable specific groups in the population or all citizens to opt out of social policy schemes. The introduction of opting out might be complete or partial. Full opting out allows individuals to completely abandon an insurance scheme or social policy. Depending on the regulations, individuals might replace the previously compulsory public scheme with a private insurance, or might decide not to cover the risk formerly insured at all. Partial opting out refers to situations in which individuals are allowed to abandon their participation in parts of the benefit schemes or insurances. For instance, in some countries possibilities have been created to cancel coverage for specific treatments like fertility treatment or physiotherapy, or to opt for lower benefits after retirement from the public pension scheme.

Thomson and Mossialos (2006) present two arguments in favour of opting out. First, based on economic theory regarding consumer choice, it might be argued that the threat of voluntary exit from the public scheme will be sufficient to stimulate competition between public and private insurers, leading to greater responsiveness and increased efficiency. A second argument is that encouraging individuals to opt for private coverage will ease pressure on the government budget and allow public finances to be spent on improving the provision of services and benefits for poorer people. This requires those who opt out of public coverage to continue to contribute to public resources – for example, through taxation.

When the introduction of free choice also creates exit options for participants in social policies, this might undermine the universal or near-universal coverage of social policy schemes. Therefore, it is important to reflect on the consequences of the introduction of opting out. This chapter analyses to what extent opting out has been introduced in the domains of health insurance, pensions and unemployment benefits, and with what kinds of effects. In the next section, I will deal with adverse selection as one of the most important drawbacks of enabling opting out.

Adverse Selection and Solidarity

From an individual's point of view, it is rational to pool one's own risks with those of other people who are less at risk than oneself. However, if everyone has perfect information on risks and everyone reasons in the same way, people would end up pooling risks only with people who are running the same risks as themselves. Principles of insufficient information lead everyone to assume that they are as much at risk as everyone else, and everyone agrees to pool their risks with other people's on equal terms (Goodin 2001: 142).

Enabling the opting out from insurance or benefit schemes creates the risk of adverse selection. Adverse selection refers to the theoretical tendency for low-risk individuals to avoid or drop out of voluntary insurance pools, with the result that insurance pools can be expected to contain a disproportionate percentage of high-risk individuals (Baker 2001: 2). Where there is a choice of more than one type of insurance or benefit 'plan', plans offering a more generous level of benefits and/or a lower level of cost-sharing will attract individuals with a higher risk in the situation at which the plan is aimed. In response to the ensuing risk segmentation, plans with a concentration of high-risk participants must raise their premiums, provoking low-risks to switch to cheaper plans or forgo cover altogether. This leads to further premium rises and exacerbates the problem of segmentation (Thomson and Mossialos 2006: 316). Therefore, processes of adverse selection seriously threaten principles of solidarity. The chapter analyses the extent to which adverse selection might be observed in modern welfare states as a consequence of the introduction of exit options.

As has been stated in the introduction to this chapter, the empirical descriptions focus on three issues: (1) the extent to which exit options have been introduced in the domains of health insurances, unemployment schemes and pensions; (2) the extent to which these exit options actually are used by people; and (3) the extent to which adverse selection has occurred. The following sections discuss recent developments in these issues in the four countries that serve as cases in this chapter: the Netherlands, Spain, Sweden and the UK.

The Introduction of Opting Out in Health Insurance

According to Mossialos and Thomson (2002: 20), public policy in EU member states historically has aimed to preserve the principle of health care funded by the state or social insurance and made available to all citizens, regardless of ability to pay. This has resulted in health-care systems with high levels of public expenditure, near universal coverage, mandatory participation, and the provision of comprehensive benefits. However, health insurance is an area that is discussed frequently in many European countries. These discussions concern attempts to control the costs of health care, as well as attempts to increase the quality and responsiveness of health-care institutions. Aimed at the latter goal, free choice between public and private providers, between different insurers and between different coverage packages has been introduced in several European countries. The introduction of free choice might also mean that full or partial opting out has been enabled in health insurance systems that previously were mandatory. Therefore, the area of health insurance is of importance for the central theme of this chapter.

Institutional framework

In this section, I will briefly discuss the institutional framework, and its recent changes, of health insurances in the Netherlands, Spain, Sweden and the UK. Table 1 gives an overview of the key features of the organization of health insurance in the four countries and the possibilities for opting out. In the remainder of the section I will elaborate on this.

In the Netherlands, until 2005 high earners were not covered by the statutory health insurance and could take up a voluntary health insurance. Most of the high earners did this. However, as of 2006, all residents of the Netherlands are subject to the mandatory basic health insurance. This covers most medical treatments and is implemented by private insurance companies. In addition, people may take up additional insurance for treatments that are not covered by the basic insurance. A vast majority – 92 per cent of the Dutch insurees – have taken up additional insurance. Interestingly, since the introduction of the Health Insurance Act (HIA) in 2006, the coverage of treatments in the basic insurance has been slowly but gradually expanded.

The Spanish national health insurance system is completely financed out of taxes. The public system offers just about universal coverage. Civil servants are the only public insured that enjoy the privilege of being able to choose their provider of care between the public national health service and any of the private insurance companies that want to enter the scheme. About 11 per cent of the population buys voluntary health insurance in Spain. In most cases it corresponds to the supplementary type: it is bought on top of the public

Table 1

Health insurance schemes in four countries

	Health insurance system	Target group	Full opting out possibilities	Partial opting out possibilities	Alternatives
The Netherlands	Mandatory basic insurance	All residents	None	By not participating in complementary insurance	Complementary (92% have taken up complementary insurance)
Spain	Tax-financed public health service	Salaried workers and persons assimilated thereto (pensioners and residents with insufficient means of existence)	Civil servants		Substitute Complementary Supplementary
Sweden	Tax-financed public health service	All residents	None		Complementary Supplementary
United Kingdom	Tax-financed public health service	All persons 'ordinarily resident' in the UK	None		Supplementary

Sources: MISSOC, OECD (2004).

coverage and it essentially provides cover for faster access and increased consumer choice. For most, but not all, people that buy private insurance it means having duplicate coverage (Rodriguez and Stoyanova 2004).

In Sweden, the degree of public financing within the system decreased from well above 90 per cent in the late 1980s down to 80 per cent at the end of the century. This was mostly accounted for by the rise in patient fees, which grew by 30 per cent between 1993 and 1997. In addition to this, the number of private health insurance holders grew during the same period from 23,000 in 1990 to 115,000 in 2000. In conjunction with increasing numbers of for-profit care providers catering to the privately insured, this development has given rise to a debate as to whether privately insured patients should be allowed to 'jump the queue' (Blomqvist 2004: 147).

Health care in the UK is predominantly state-financed and delivered by the National Health Service (NHS). However, while approximately 85 per cent of funding comes from the public purse, the use of private health-care services is rising. While politicians have stressed their commitment to tax-financed free hospital care, policy change has reduced eligibility for publicly provided treatment, increased co-payments for dental and ophthalmic services, and pharmaceuticals, and reduced the payments made to independent contractors who provide state-financed dental care. These changes have been accompanied by a growth in the importance of the private sector in the provision of health care in the UK (Propper 2000).

Adverse selection in health insurance

The issue of adverse selection in health-care systems forms an interesting puzzle because of the wide variety of systems and their complex interactions. In theory, there are at least three situations that might illustrate the probability of adverse selection in health insurance: the co-existence of a public health system and a supplementary ('double coverage') private insurance system, complementary insurances and substitutive insurance. Two of these situations can be found within the original sample of the four countries: double coverage in the UK and complementary insurance in the Netherlands. As there are no experiences with substitutive insurance in any of the four countries, I will rely on experiences in Germany to assess its consequences for adverse selection. Table 2 gives a short overview of the findings.

Adverse selection in supplementary health insurance. In the United Kingdom, private medical insurance is mostly used to obtain quicker access to hospital treatments of better quality compared to the public treatments. In this situation, adverse selection presupposes a positive relation between risk and participation in private insurance: people with higher risks will more easily decide to take up private coverage. In their analysis of supplementary private medical insurance in the United Kingdom, Olivella and Vera-Hernández (2006) found strong evidence of adverse selection. They compared the probabilities of hospitalization of those who buy private medical insurance and those who receive private insurance as a fringe benefit. They found that these probabilities are significantly higher for the first group. This implies that people who

Table 2

Adverse selection in health insurance

	Empirical evidence	Adverse selection	Effects
Supplementary	United Kingdom (Olivella and Vera-Hernández 2006)	Yes	People with supplementary insurance have higher risks than people with only public insurance
Complementary	The Netherlands (Roos and Schut 2008)	Not significant	Large proportion of people (>90%) do have complementary insurance
Substitutive	Germany (OECD 2004; Nuscheler and Knaus 2005)	Yes	Privately insured tend to be younger and healthier

are in a position to make a choice between public and private coverage, deliberately and correctly assess their own risk profile when making a decision. This leads to the conclusion that in supplementary health systems, adverse selection is possible. In relation to the central theme of this chapter, we therefore might conclude that although the UK's health insurance system does not offer exit options, there is evidence that adverse selection might occur if exit options were to be introduced. Individuals seem to be able to assess their own risk profiles and adjust their health insurances to these risk profiles.

Adverse selection in complementary health insurance. Out of the four countries that are analysed in this chapter, the Dutch case offers the best possibilities to assess the occurrence of adverse selection in complementary insurance. A trend that might be expected is that when certain treatments are excluded from basic coverage, people with a higher risk for the diseases that might need this treatment take up additional insurance covering these treatments. Conclusions from the Dutch case on this issue can be briefly stated: (1) there has been a gradual extension of treatments that are covered by the basic insurance, and (2) a very high proportion (over 90 per cent of the insurees) do have additional health insurance. There is no information available on the risks of prevalence of diseases in the people without additional health care.

In contrast to the basic insurance, there is no obligation for acceptation, nor are there any restrictions for differentiations in premiums. Almost all the insured have the same provider for basic insurance and additional insurance. This is not obligatory, but insurers are allowed to charge additional fees to those insured with additional insurances only at their company. Therefore, the policies for additional insurance might also serve as a tool for selection for the basic insurance. There are clear indications that this is the case, as insurance companies offer reduced premiums for additional insurance for low-risk groups. For instance, members of sport clubs may qualify for reduced rates (Roos and Schut 2008).

Adverse selection in substitutive health insurance. Unfortunately for this analysis, none of the countries that we focus on in this chapter has a significant substitutive system. This limits the opportunity to reflect on the effect of substitutive systems. However, concerning the consequences of substitutive health care, we might learn from the experiences in Germany, which is a country with substitutive health insurance. In Germany high earners are able to opt out of the public insurance and take up private insurance. It appears that in Germany the privately insured tend to be younger and healthier than the publicly insured. As younger people usually need less medical treatment, this deprives the public risk pool of some of the less expensive risks (OECD 2004: 285). Nuscheler and Knaus (2005) state that this might be attributed to the lower switching costs for healthier people. Since low-risk consumers are – due to lower switching costs – more likely to switch, the resulting flow towards substitutive insurance improved the private insurance's risk pool.

Health insurance: conclusions

None of the four countries that have been discussed has introduced exit options in health insurance in recent years. Rather the contrary: the only country with a system of voluntary insurance for a large part of the population, the Netherlands, introduced compulsory basic insurance for the entire population in 2006. In Europe, the only country that offers the choice of opting out of health insurance is Germany. Therefore, we cannot conclude that a shift towards opting out has been introduced in recent years in Europe.

So, to analyse the issue of adverse selection in health insurance, it is necessary to go beyond the four countries that serve as cases in this chapter. Then it appears that adverse selection primarily occurs in substitutive systems. In supplementary systems, the supplementary insurances seem to attract people with higher medical costs, whereas in countries with large complementary systems, the risk pool resembles the total population.

The Introduction of Opting Out in Pension Schemes

The central question of this chapter is to what extent different European countries have introduced elements of 'free choice' into their social policies and what consequences this introduction has had on the coverage for several social risks. In the previous section, I dealt with the issue of health insurance. In this section, I will focus on the introduction of free choice in pension systems in those countries. While there are several risks connected with old age – primarily related to health issues – in this chapter I focus on the risk of loss of income after retirement. Retirement might be considered as a logical consequence of decreasing productivity when people get older. In almost all modern countries, pensions serve as a mode of income after retirement. These pensions may take many different shapes: they might be financed by general taxes or by contributions from workers and employers; they might be based on the pay-as-you-go system whereby state benefits to retirees are paid out of contributions from current workers, or they might be (partly) based on private contributions. In all cases, costs of the pensions are based on the size of the benefits and estimations of the number of years that people live after retirement.

This section is structured similarly to the previous section. First, I will analyse if possibilities of opting-out have been introduced in the four countries, and which ones. Next, I will focus on the consequences this has had for the pension coverage in these countries, and finally I will assess the consequences of opting-out for the overall risk pool.

Institutional framework

Pension systems usually consist of multiple pillars. The first pillar is considered as a safety net with universal coverage that aims to prevent poverty in old age. This first pillar is provided by the public sector. These first-pillar pension benefits can be either flat-rate or targeted to older people with low incomes (OECD 2007). The second pillar plays an 'insurance' role. It aims to provide retirees with an adequate income relative to their previous earnings. In nearly all countries this second pillar is mandatory, as is the first pillar. Usually, second-pillar pensions are forms of occupational welfare negotiated between employers and employees. The third pillar is an additional, voluntary system that people can use to supplement their income after retirement.

Considering the central question of this chapter, there are several reforms in pension systems that might facilitate full or partial 'opting out'. In theory, there could be four roads through which opting out of pension schemes is possible (see also Disney *et al.* 1999):

1. opening up the mandatory first pillar;
2. gradually decreasing the benefits that retirees will receive from the first pillar, thereby creating opportunities for additional coverage from voluntary second- or third-pillar schemes;
3. abolishing the mandatory character of second-pillar schemes;
4. gradually decreasing the benefits that retirees will receive from the mandatory second pillar, thereby creating opportunities for additional coverage from voluntary third-pillar schemes.

Concerning the first possibility, it appears that out of the four countries that are discussed in this chapter, only Spain offers specific groups of employees the possibility to exit the first pillar. Whereas in the three other countries coverage of the first pillar is 100 per cent, in Spain this is 89 per cent. Civil servants working for the central government or the justice system and people working for the armed forces are exempted from the regular, state-funded first-pillar pension. The compulsory special schemes for these groups show large similarities to the first-pillar pensions in Spain (Social Protection Committee 2006). When discussing the second possibility, it is necessary to be aware of the enormous variations in pension schemes across countries. However, the European Union's attempt to assess and compare pension schemes in various Social Protection Reports (see, for instance, EC 2006) provides some helpful material. Table 3 presents gross and net replacement rates of pension benefits in 2004 and 2050.[1] This table illustrates the impact of current pension reforms on prospective coverage rates, and identifies shifts from the first to the second and third pillars. Concerning this issue, Greve (2007) argues that the shift from first-pillar mandatory pensions to occupational pensions might increase the inequalities between those inside and outside the labour market.

None of the countries that takes a central place in this chapter has introduced formal opting-out options, neither have they significantly lowered mandatory pension provision, which might be considered as possibilities for partial opting out. If the pension systems are analysed in detail, some elements of the introduction of exit options can be observed in the UK and Sweden. Recent reforms in the Netherlands were aimed at a shift from end salaries to average lifetime salaries in the second-pillar schemes. In Spain a wide variety of private and occupational complementary pension plans exist, but considering the generosity of the mandatory first-pillar benefits, their importance is rather limited.

The Swedish case is rather interesting. Whereas the statutory pension scheme is by far the most important pension provision, it is far more flexible than other first-pillar schemes. Pension rights may be drawn starting at age 61, and there is no definite retirement age. A rate of 25, 50, 75 or 100 per cent of the pension may be drawn. The decrease in replacement rate shown in table 3 is caused by the Swedish answer to the challenge of an ageing population: cohorts who retire in 2050 would need to work for 44 years, up to the age of 69, to achieve the same replacement rates as those who retire in 2005.

The UK's first-pillar pension consists of a flat-rate basic pension and an earnings-related additional pension: the State Second Pension. Individuals can choose to opt out of the State Second Pension when they transfer to an occupational or personal scheme providing equivalent or better benefits than

Table 3

Pension replacement rates (EU15 countries)

	Total net replacement rate		Total gross replacement rate		Gross replacement rate 1st pillar		Gross replacement rate 2nd and 3rd pillar	
	2004	2050	2004	2050	2004	2050	2004	2050
Netherlands	92	90	71	69	30	30	41*	39*
Spain	97	92	91	85	91	85		
Sweden	71	57	68	56	53	40	15	15
UK	82	85	66	69	17	19	50	50

*Negligible proportion.
Source: European Commmission (2006).

the statutory scheme. Some 60 per cent of the employed are in such con-
tracted-out schemes.

Adverse selection in pensions

When using the concept of adverse selection in the context of pensions, in
fact we are discussing issues of life and death. People who expect to live relatively long benefit most from pension schemes, whereas people who think they
could die young might want to minimize their contribution to pension schemes
in return for lower pension benefits after retirement. Although the proliferation of 'life expectancy tests' on the internet suggests otherwise, there is an
enormous amount of uncertainty concerning life expectancy at the individual
level. Some risk factors clearly reduce life expectancy: smoking, short-lived
parents, and being overweight are examples of these. There are two aspects
that mitigate the impact of knowledge about risk factors on an individual's
pension decisions. First, the overwhelming majority of known risk factors are
probabilistic instead of deterministic, with the exception of some genetic
diseases. This implies that even the presence of severe risk factors does not
block out the possibility of a long life in retirement. Second, most risk factors
have only a moderate effect on life expectancy. Smoking is one of the most
severe risk factors for early death, and reduces the life expectancy by 5 to 10
years. The effect of most other risk factors is substantially lower (Hamermesh
and Hamermesh 1983). So the conclusion here is that although people may
have opportunities to exit mandatory pension schemes, adverse selection is
not likely to occur in pensions as a deliberate individual strategy.

What might happen is that people decide to switch providers for other
reasons than a deliberate assessment of their individual risks, for instance
because of the efficiency of private rather than public pension providers.
When the risk profiles of people who decide to switch from pension suppliers
differs from the overall risk pool, this might also create processes of adverse
selection. However, as we have seen in the previous section, the proportion
of people switching from their pension provider is rather low.

Pensions: conclusions

The introduction of elements of free choice in pension schemes has not created
possibilities to exit formally from mandatory pension schemes in the four countries that have been analysed. Only the UK offers partial opting out of the State
Second Pension. As far as adverse selection is concerned, the conclusion is that
this is no real issue in the pension schemes of the EU15 countries, including the
countries that have been closely analysed. There are only limited possibilities
to opt out, and decreasing benefits are not compensated for on a significant
scale by private pension plans with specific risk profiles.

The Introduction of Opting Out in Unemployment Schemes

Unemployment is a social risk that to some extent differs from other social
risks: it tends not to be distributed evenly among a population, but hits larger

groups of employees in cycles. It might hit employees in specific sectors that lose competitive advantage, or might spread throughout the entire labour force in times of economic recession. Therefore, in the 1920s and 1930s two types of unemployment schemes replaced the early unemployment schemes run by trade unions: the so-called Ghent system, which provided public subsidies to voluntary trade union-run systems and systems of compulsory unemployment insurance (see Clasen and Viebrock 2008). In contemporary welfare states, membership in unemployment insurance is mandatory for the large majority of employees, and national schemes are run solely by the state or by the state in cooperation with social partners. Voluntary unemployment insurance administered by trade union-linked funds survived only in Denmark, Sweden and Finland (Clasen and Viebrock 2008; see also Holmlund 1998). In the section below, I will briefly describe the key characteristics of the unemployment insurances in the Netherlands, Spain, Sweden and the UK, and identify to what extent opting out is possible. Next, I will focus on the way exit options are actually used, and on the impact of exit options on adverse selection.

Institutional framework

The Dutch Unemployment Insurance Act (WW) insures employees against the financial consequences of unemployment. The WW is financed by contributions from employers and employees, and is compulsory for all employees. The Institute for Employee Benefit Schemes (UWV) is responsible for the implementation. The insurance provides a benefit of 70 per cent of initial salaries. The Spanish unemployment insurance very much resembles the Dutch system. It is also compulsory for all employees, and also offers benefits at 70 per cent of the initial salary. There are no options to fully or partially exit the unemployment insurance.

As has been stated in the introduction to this section, the Swedish unemployment insurance is voluntary. It offers a flat-rate benefit to employees not in voluntary unemployment insurance, and a benefit of 80 per cent of initial earnings to those who participate. Finally, in the UK the compulsory unemployment insurance only offers a flat-rate benefit for all employed persons except for married women who chose before April 1977 not to be insured. This flat-rate benefit is at the level of 10 per cent of the average salary.

Adverse selection in unemployment insurance

Vaughan and Vaughan (2001) argue that an individual's options for managing the risks of unemployment are very limited. The primary means of dealing with unemployment comes via state unemployment insurance programmes, which tend to be limited in both amount and duration. The authors state that for most individuals, risk retention and reduction are the only means available for dealing with the unemployment risk. The only means to reduce the risk is through acquisition of education or specialized skills, or by selecting a career with little fluctuation in employment levels.

Adverse selection is an issue that is frequently brought forward in connection with unemployment insurance. Chiu and Karni (1998: 820) illustrate the occurrence of adverse selection with the case of the Canadian firm 'Career Guard', a private, additional unemployment scheme. In this case it appeared that people who took up this insurance had a significantly higher risk of getting fired than average employees. This illustrative case is supported more generally by Kim's analysis of social risk perceptions and support for unemployment insurance. He concludes that support for unemployment insurance is higher among people in economic sectors characterized by a high probability of unemployment (Kim 2007: 250).

Ejrnaes and Hochguertel (2008) conducted a study of Danish panel data on self-employed and unemployment insurance. Their question was not whether self-employed people use their status to circumvent social insurances, but their findings do provide some insights on this issue. They came to two conclusions. First, the self-employed were not primarily interested in unemployment insurance, but participated because of the early retirement scheme that the Danish unemployment insurance offered. Insurees have the option of participating in an early retirement scheme, unavailable to non-insurees. The second conclusion was that self-employed people with unemployment insurance become unemployed more often than those without unemployment insurance. Ejrnaes and Hochguertel argue that moral hazard is responsible for this. However, it might also be the case that people participating in unemployment insurance know that they have a relatively high risk of unemployment, because of personal or business characteristics. Anyway, the main conclusion concerning this issue is that the self-employed do not choose their self-employed status because of risk management strategies.

Clasen and Viebrock (2008: 438) come to a similar conclusion concerning the role of adverse selection in Denmark and Sweden. They conclude that 'adverse risk selection is avoided by relatively generous benefits and low direct costs, both of which make membership in voluntary funds attractive'.

Unemployment insurance: conclusions

None of the four countries has recently introduced possibilities for opting out from unemployment insurance. In Sweden, voluntary unemployment insurance is a key feature of the system. However, a very large proportion of the employees participate in voluntary unemployment insurance, thus mitigating the risk of adverse selection. However, from other research it appears that unemployment insurance in theory is vulnerable to the risk of adverse selection, primarily because insurees to some extent have knowledge about their own risk profiles.

Conclusions

In this chapter, I have tried to identify to what extent the introduction of free choice in social policies has led to the introduction of exit options in these policies. This question is relevant because individuals' decisions to opt out of social policies might have collective effects for the sustainability of these

Table 4

Conclusions

		The Netherlands	Spain	Sweden	UK
Health insurance	Full opting out	No	No	No	No
	Partial opting out	By not participating in additional insurance	No	No	By taking up complementary health insurance
	Adverse selection	No evidence	No evidence	No evidence	The contrary: people with complementary health insurance tend to have higher health costs
Pension scheme	Full opting out	No	No	No	No
	Partial opting out	Declining replacement rate might be complemented with voluntary schemes	No	Flexibility in age of retirement and height of benefits	Yes
	Adverse selection	No evidence	No evidence	No evidence	No evidence
Unemployment insurance	Full opting out	No	No	Yes	No
	Partial opting out	No	No	No	No
	Adverse selection	No evidence	No evidence	No evidence	No evidence

policies. When the people deciding to exit are those who are 'better off' in the distribution of risks, the overall risk profile of the people that stay in the policy worsens, creating a vicious circle of increasing contributions and more people deciding to exit.

This chapter has set out to achieve three goals: (1) to identify to what extent exit options are available and have increased in recent years in European welfare states; (2) to assess to what extent these exit options are actually used; and (3) to analyse if these exit options lead to processes of adverse selection. To achieve these goals, four countries were selected that form illustrations of different types of European welfare states. Table 4 presents a condensed version of the most important conclusions of the analysis in this chapter.

The analysis in this chapter only allows one, if somewhat unsatisfactory, conclusion: there is no trend towards the introduction of exit options in social policies in the European welfare states that have been studied. And even if we go beyond the four cases that took a central place, hardly any of the other EU15 states have introduced possibilities for opting out of pension schemes, health insurances or unemployment insurances. Perhaps rather surprisingly, in some cases – for instance Dutch health insurance – initiatives have been undertaken to extend the coverage or introduce mandatory universal coverage instead of exit options. Moreover, in the cases where exit options exist, no convincing evidence has been found of processes of adverse selection.

Does this imply that opting out is not an issue to worry about in social policies? To some extent, it seems that, indeed, in most European welfare states the risk of adverse selection is tackled by mandatory universal coverage of social policies or highly attractive voluntary insurances that attract almost universal coverage. However, this chapter has also shown several examples of processes of adverse selection and their impact on social policies from beyond the four countries that took a central place in this chapter. These examples illustrate the reality of processes of adverse selection in the domain of social policy, and its potential danger for solidarity. Especially in an era in which knowledge of risks is an important asset, this underlines the necessity to monitor closely the introduction of opting out and its effects.

Note

1. Theoretical replacement rates are dependent on the assumptions with which they are calculated. These calculations are based on a person who has qualified for full pensions, earning 100 per cent of average earnings, retiring in 2005, or retiring in 2050 with changes in conditions that have been implemented to date. Gross replacement rates refer to the relation of salary earnings just before retirement and pension income before taxes; net replacement rates refer to the relation of salary earnings just before retirement and pension income after taxes.

References

Baker, T. (2001), *Containing the Promise of Insurance: Adverse Selection and Risk Classification*, Hartford: University of Connecticut School of Law Articles and Working Papers.
Blomqvist, P. (2004), The choice revolution: privatization of the Swedish welfare services in the 1990s, *Social Policy & Administration*, 38, 2: 139–55.

Chiu, W. H. and Karni, E. (1998), Endogenous adverse selection and unemployment insurance, *Journal of Political Economy*, 106, 4: 806–27.

Clasen, J. and Viebrock, E. (2008), Voluntary unemployment insurance and trade union membership: investigating the connections in Denmark and Sweden, *Journal of Social Policy*, 37, 3: 433–51.

Disney, R., Palacios, R. and Whitehouse, E. (1999), *Individual Choice of Pension Arrangement as a Pension Reform Strategy*, Working Paper series, no. 8, London: Institute for Fiscal Studies.

Ejrnaes, M. and Hochguertel, S. (2008), *Entrepreneurial Moral Hazard in Income Insurance*, Amsterdam: Tinbergen Institute.

European Commission (EC) (2006), *Adequate and Sustainable Pensions: Synthesis Report 2006*, Brussels: EC.

Goodin, R. E. (2001), Review of 'The New Social Question: Rethinking the Welfare State', *Economics and Philosophy*, 17: 140–5.

Greener, I. (2008), Choice or voice? Introduction to the themed section, *Social Policy and Society*, 7, 2: 197–200.

Greve, B. (2007), *Occupational Welfare: Winners and Losers*, Cheltenham: Edward Elgar.

Hamermesh, D. S. and Hamermesh, F. W. (1983), Does perception of life expectancy reflect health knowledge? *American Journal of Public Health*, 73, 8: 911–14.

Holmlund, B. (1998), Unemployment insurance in theory and practice, *Scandinavian Journal of Economics*, 100, 1: 113–41.

Kim, W. (2007), Social risk and social insurance: political demand for unemployment insurance, *Rationality and Society*, 19: 229–54.

Mossialos, E. and Thomson, S. M. (2002), Voluntary health insurance in the European Union: a critical assessment, *International Journal of Health Services*, 32, 1: 19–88.

Nuscheler, R. and Knaus, T. (2005), Risk selection in the German public health insurance system, *Health Economics*, 14, 12: 1253–71.

OECD (2004), *Towards High-performing Health Systems*, Paris: OECD.

OECD (2007), *Pensions at a Glance*, Paris: OECD.

Olivella, P. and Vera-Hernández, M. (2006), *Testing for Adverse Selection into Private Medical Insurance*, working paper 06/02, London: Institute for Fiscal Studies.

Pollitt, C. (2003), *The Essential Public Manager*, Maidenhead: Open University Press.

Propper, C. (2000), The demand for private health care in the UK, *Journal of Health Economics*, 19, 6: 855–76.

Rodriguez, M. and Stoyanova, A. (2004), The effect of private insurance access on the choice of GP/specialist and public/private provider in Spain, *Health Economics*, 13, 7: 689–703.

Roos, A. F. and Schut, F. T. (2008), *Evaluatie aanvullende en collectieve verzekeringen 2008* [Evaluation of supplementary and collective insurances 2008], Rotterdam: IBMG.

Rosanvallon, P. (2000), *The New Social Question: Rethinking the Welfare State*, Princeton, NJ: Princeton University Press.

Social Protection Committee (2006), *Current and Prospective Theoretical Pension Replacement Rates*, report by the Indicators Sub-Group, Brussels.

Thomson, S. and Mossialos, E. (2006), Choice of public or private health insurance: learning from the experience of Germany and the Netherlands, *Journal of European Social Policy*, 16, 4: 315–27.

Vaughan, E. and Vaughan, T. (2001), *Essentials of Risk Management and Insurance*, New York: John Wiley.

9
Freedom of Choice through the Promotion of Gender Equality
Steven Saxonberg

Introduction

In recent years, the issue of 'freedom of choice' has become increasingly prevalent in the debates on public policy in general and welfare policy in particular. Although it originally grew out of the neo-liberal discourse on the need for privatization and retrenchment, even more social liberal and social democratically oriented theorists began claiming that a process of individualization has been taking place, in which preferences for career, lifestyle and caring choices have become more pluralized (Beck 1992, 2001; Giddens 1991). Both our wants and needs have become more diversified as we have moved away from the assembly line towards jobs that allow for greater work-time flexibility, working partially or fully at home, the possibility to work part-time, etc. Thus, they claim traditional standardized welfare policies cannot meet the needs of citizens as well as in the past.

This chapter focuses on family policy because, as feminist theorists have noted, no policies have greater influence over gender roles than family policies (i.e. Lewis 1993; Sainsbury 1994), which in turn means that family policies influence almost every aspect of our daily lives, from the manner in which we relate to our romantic partners, to our ability to have careers and compete on the job market and the way we raise our children.

Family policy also presents an interesting case because some basic aspects of it, such as parental-leave insurance, cannot emerge from a free market, but rather by their nature require state intervention. Private insurance providers would not be able to make a profit without any state support or regulation, as they would expect their clients to have children and thus demand payment rather early in their adult lives after only paying insurance premiums for a few years. Then the clients would discontinue their membership in the insurance scheme almost immediately after having the number of children that they want. Thus no long buffer period exists for most adults in which they might be expected to pay insurance fees without demanding any benefits in return.

Family policies also bring up the long-standing debate on positive and negative freedom in a rather special light. Free-market supporters using the notion of negative freedom would claim that the way to maximize choice in society is to let markets take care of everything, while social democrats and social liberals can argue perhaps more clearly than in many other cases that considerable conflict exists between what choices the market provides and what choices *could* be available if the state were to pursue policies that increase our freedom of choice. For example, in the United States it is common to ask mothers whether they breastfeed their infants, while in Europe it is *obvious* that the mother breastfeeds the child unless health reasons prevent it. This difference does not arise because American mothers have different preferences than European mothers – American mothers are just as aware that it is healthier for the infant to get milk from the mother than from baby formulas – rather, the difference is that in almost all European countries paid maternity and parental leaves exist that allow mothers to stay at home for usually at least half a year, while American mothers did not even get the right to a short three-month unpaid leave until the courts ruled in the 1990s that mothers were entitled to a 'sick leave', because they were not physically capable of working after having a child. Many mothers cannot afford this unpaid leave and others are afraid that taking even this short leave would gravely affect their careers. Another striking example is the case of a female doctoral student in the United States, who told me that she had recently become pregnant and when her adviser found out he tried to persuade her to get an abortion, otherwise she would lose her scholarship! In European countries, by contrast, mothers have the right to return to their jobs after going on maternity leave, even if they are doctoral students at a university. So here differences in family policy can literally become a question of life itself!

The main argument of this chapter is that *family policies which promote gender equality also increase freedom of choice more than either laissez-faire liberal or conservative policies*. They do so by increasing the amount of available choices to both the mothers and fathers by making it easier for women to choose to have careers while still having children and by making it easier for men to choose to spend time with their children. Even women who are not interested in having a career have a greater number of options available under social democratic regime-types that promote gender equality than under the liberal or conservative alternatives, as such policies still make it easier for them to choose to have children given the economic constraints that make it difficult for most families to live on one income. In fact, given the budget constraints that exist, then social democratic policies that aim to promote gender equality have in practice been more generous even towards women who would prefer to stay at home with their children full-time and not work at all. However, I will also argue that the question is more complicated than simply whether policies promote gender equality or not, because even among policies that promote gender equality, one can develop policies that are more flexible and give more freedom of choice, or policies that are less flexible and give less freedom of choice, in the sense of giving more or less option of how parents can divide their time between work and family.

Despite these rather straightforward arguments, two factors complicate the analysis of freedom of choice, although, if one includes these elements in the analysis, they strengthen the argument that measures which promote gender equality increase freedom of choice. First, a possible conflict can arise between long-term and short-term freedom of choice. In some cases, policies that place some limits on freedom of choice in the short run (such as reserving parental leave months only for the father even if he would 'prefer' to work) can actually increase freedom of choice in the long run. Second, if one takes into account structural factors, such as cultural norms that might, for example, prevent men from making the choices that they would have made without these constraints, then policies that reserve parental leave months only for fathers could actually increase freedom of choice also by fighting against structural factors and making men realize more clearly what they would 'really' want to choose if they had not felt constrained by these cultural norms.

I break this chapter down into five sections: (1) maternity leave policies; (2) paternity leave policies; (3) the flexibility of parental leaves; (4) day-care policies; and (5) policies towards non-nuclear families. It should also be noted that most of the Scandinavian examples will concentrate on Sweden, because as Sainsbury (1999) shows, its policies go farther in promoting gender equality than Denmark, Norway or Finland, while most of the examples of conservative policies will be based on Germany, both because that country has often been considered the ideal-typical conservative welfare state and because its recent moves towards the Swedish model help indicate the problems that the conservative model faces today.

Maternity Leaves

Hakim (2000) built upon the individualization hypothesis to develop her preference theory, in which she basically argues that family policies can have only very limited influence on behaviour, because women in post-industrial societies have developed different preferences. One group of women is 'career-oriented', and will always want to work regardless of policies; a second group is 'family-oriented', and will always want to give priority to having a family over working regardless of policies. Consequently, only the third group of 'adaptable' women will adapt their choices to changes in family policies.

A problem with this line of reasoning is that Hakim herself considers the group of adaptable women to be the largest (representing about 60 per cent of all women), which implies that policies in fact will have impact on choices. Another problem with Hakim's argument is that she claims that gender equality is not possible because while women have different preferences, virtually all men have the same preference for placing their careers over their families. As a result, policies cannot influence men to share in raising children. Rather than investigate this hypothesis empirically by using survey data as she does for women, she merely assumes this to be the case. She also refers to Sweden as proof that policies promoting gender equality cannot induce men to change their behaviour to stay at home with their children. This is also a rather strange conclusion, given the fact that the percentage of parental leave time in that country has been progressively increasing over the last two decades and has now surpassed the 20 per cent level (SCB 2008).

Despite the drawbacks of Hakim's arguments, what is interesting for present purposes is that if it is true that women have preferences in line with what Hakim writes, then policies promoting gender equality would still actually provide more freedom of choice than traditional liberal or conservative policies. For the career-oriented group, generous social democratic policies that encourage fathers to stay at home and give easy access to quality day care allow career-oriented women the *choice* of having children without having to give up their careers. If the father of the children stays at home most of the time during the first year or years and then the children attend day care, then women who do not want to give up successful careers for their families would no longer be required to do so.

Meanwhile, for the largest group, comprising adaptable women who are interested in both working and having families, policies that encourage fathers to stay at home for a while, provide easy access to day care and also provide generous leave provisions for mothers for their period at home also make it much easier for these adaptable women to balance work and family life. While conservative policies that support the male-breadwinner model might force these women against their will to become housewives and completely give up their careers, and liberal, laissez-faire policies might make it difficult for these women to spend any time at all at home with their children, the Scandinavian types of policies that promote gender equality allow the adaptable women to stay at home for a while and receive generous leave payments (80 per cent of previous salary in Sweden, for example), but also make it easier for them to return to their jobs since they are guaranteed the right to come back to the same job and position if they return within one and a half years.

The most ambivalent case concerns Hakim's family-oriented group. One could argue that conservative policies that promote motherhood and induce mothers to become housewives would be the preferred policy for this group. Regardless of whether that would be true, social democratic policies that promote gender equality still provide the family-oriented group with more choice than the liberal, laissez-faire model. In a purely liberal model mothers do not receive any paid parental leave at all, so family-oriented women might find that even if they want to stay at home, they cannot afford to do so; in some cases, they might decide they cannot afford to have children at all. It is worth noting that the International Social Survey Programme survey on the family shows that, among European countries, the Netherlands was the only country in which fewer than 70 per cent of the female respondents believed that women need to work to support their families.[1] In the market-liberal USA the total was over 86 per cent. Thus, even women who have family-oriented values often find that they must work, so social democratic policies that make it easier for them to balance work and family life will make it easier for women to have children than under the liberal model, since they will at least get some paid leave time to stay at home and then will still be able to utilize cheap public childcare services when they feel that they must return to work for economic reasons.

Of course, even if family-oriented women have greater freedom of choice under the gender equality model than the liberal one, they still might prefer a purely conservative model that would enable them to be completely financially independent from the labour market, so that they could become housewives, while the Nordic model only makes it easy for women to stay at home for a couple of years. For example, in Sweden parents receive 13 months of insurance-based leave at 80 per cent of their salaries, with two months reserved solely for the mother and two solely for the father, but in practice parents often stay at home for a longer period by utilizing less than 100 per cent of the daily payment. For example, they can choose to stay at home twice as long for a total of 26 months and receive 50 per cent of the benefits per day (which amounts to 40 per cent of their salary). Some strains of feminism argue against the abolition of gender roles and instead claim that women *should* be the main carers, *but* they should be given a 'normal' salary for caring, so that they can become economically independent from their husbands. According to this view, the problem is not that women have different roles from men but rather it is that women's roles are undervalued.[2]

One obvious problem with the argument in favour of this type of 'maternal feminism' is that it would be extremely expensive. If the government were to provide mothers with a monthly salary equal to the country's average salary for their entire adult life or even 'only' for the 18-year period in which they take care of a child, the costs would be so high that they would become prohibitive, especially if one takes into account the government's loss of tax revenues from women who decide to stay at home rather than pursue careers. In practice, conservative governments have not 'succeeded' in inducing women to stay at home for longer periods with their children because their policies are not generous enough to give women the choice of staying at home; in fact they normally do not give more money for parental leaves than social democratic countries. Rather, they induce mothers to stay at home for longer periods with their children by *denying* the choice of returning earlier to work by limiting access to day care and discouraging fathers from sharing in the parental leaves. Thus, in Germany, before its recent reforms, mothers received a generous maternity leave at 100 per cent of their previous salary, but that is only slightly more generous than the 90 per cent that Sweden used to give before its economic crisis in the early 1990s and still not much more than the 80 per cent that Sweden offers today. Although 80 per cent is somewhat less generous than 100 per cent, as already noted, in Sweden mothers can receive this high level of payment for 11 months. In contrast, in the old German model mothers only received this high amount for 14 weeks, which were followed by a means-tested child-raising leave (*Erziehungsurlaub*) that paid a low, flat-rate benefit (OECD 2007). Since very few nurseries existed for children under three and many kindergartens were not open full-time (Deutsches Jugendinstitut 2008: 46), mothers often felt forced to stay at home with their children until they began school. Under such conditions, one would expect the career-oriented and adaptive women either to give up their career ambitions or their motherhood ambitions, but the question is whether this large group of around 80 per cent of the population would really be giving up its freedom of choice for the small group of 20 per cent who are family-oriented. If that were the case, then at least one group could benefit from conservative policies. But as already noted, even many family-oriented women feel that they must work to survive economically, so the conservative model that is based on *taking away* the choice of balancing work and family also takes away the possibility for many family-oriented women to choose to have children.

Since the conservative model in practice eliminates the choice for many women to balance both work and family, the only realistic choice for many women is to give up their dreams of motherhood. The resulting drop in fertility has been so great that many continental countries have been abandoning the conservative family policy model and have moved closer to the Scandinavian direction. Thus, in Germany, the Christian Democratic Chancellor (together with her party comrade who was minister of family affairs) pushed through a reform that eliminated the child-raising leave and replaced it with a one-year parental leave insurance. In addition, it provides for a two-month bonus if the father goes on leave for at least two months. The government has also committed itself to radically building up access to day care for children under three.[3] It seems that traditional, conservative, male-breadwinner policies have not been able to meet the needs of either family-oriented women or family-oriented policy-makers.

Parental Leave Policies: The Fathers

So far the argument has been that the Scandinavian types of parental leave policies that aim to promote gender equality actually provide more freedom of choice for all three of Hakim's groups of women than liberal or conservative policies, but what about men? Hakim just assumes that all men have the same preferences for careers over families without empirically investigating this issue. Yet, if it is true that our attitudes are becoming more pluralized as we move from an industrial to a post-industrial society, from modern to post-modern views and we are becoming more individualized, then why would we expect all men to have the exact same preferences about parenthood? Moreover, in contrast to Hakim's claims, policies *do* seem to influence male behaviour, as in Sweden men now account for over 20 per cent of the parental-leave time.

The question is, from the view of freedom of choice: should we be satisfied with economic incentives such as a parental leave system that provides a high level of benefits, so that families would not lose much money if the fathers stay at home even though fathers usually earn more money than mothers? In both Norway and Sweden policy-makers concluded that providing economic incentives was not enough, so they introduced a 'daddy month' in the 1990s, which reserved one of the parental leave months solely for the father. Iceland went so far as to reserve one-third of the leave time for fathers, while the Swedish government eventually added a second daddy month.

From the freedom-of-choice perspective, reserving months for fathers might seem an infringement, because it limits the ability of men to choose to continue working and have the mother stay at home, but the issue is more complicated than that for several reasons. First, even assuming that daddy months might limit the freedom of choice for some men, they could also at the same time increase the freedom of choice for women, since women have the possibility of returning to their jobs more quickly if the fathers of their children share in the parental leave time. Second, the tricky issue arises of children. Technically, infants cannot reasonably 'choose' whether or not they want their fathers to spend time at home with them, as they are too young to even comprehend the word 'choice'. For this reason, in the Swedish discourse the term 'right' is often used instead. For example, one government report proclaims: 'The child has a right to early and close contact with both parents' (Batljan *et al.* 2004: 17, my translation). Despite the usage of the term 'rights', the logic of such arguments implies that *if* infants were capable of making choices, they would choose to exercise their rights to have a father home with them.

These examples show that when it comes to freedom of choice, when the father chooses whether or not to stay at home with his children, he is also directly influencing the freedom of choice of the mother and indirectly influencing the presumed freedom of choice of the children. Yet, even leaving out these matters, the father's choice is a rather complicated issue. Feminists and Marxists have traditionally criticized the liberal view of free choice, because liberalism assumes that society is nothing but a collection of free individuals and thus ignores the structural restraints imposed by underlying power structures. These structures can hinder our choice even if we are aware of our own best interests, but they can also influence our preferences by giving us some kind of 'false consciousness'. Thus, Lukes (1974) develops the notion of 'real interests' which he defines as *the interests that we would really have if our thoughts were not manipulated by ruling power structures that in turn influence the mass media, our culture and our cultural institutions such as schools.* This view implies that, deep down, we as individuals have interests that might differ from our conscious preferences, since our preferences have been manipulated so much by socialization processes and the mass media that we think we have a certain preference (such as men thinking that they should only work and never take care of children) although we might actually prefer an alternative if we were aware of our 'real interests' (so these same men might find that they would actually prefer to spend time with their children if they had freed themselves from their manipulated socialization and actually spent time at home with their children). Of course, the notion of real interests in practice is very problematical, because the issue then arises of just who defines real interests. This leads to risks of authoritarianism as a small elite (such at the 'workers' vanguard' in communist dictatorships) decides it knows what is really in everyone's interests. This is such a complicated issue that it cannot be developed further here, but for present purposes it is enough to point out that 'preferences' as usually defined are also problematical, since many men might actual 'prefer' to spend time at home with their children if they actually had the experience of doing it (for example, by being pressured into it via daddy months), but given the cultural constraints and socialization processes that they went through, they are not aware ('conscious') that they would actually enjoy being at home with their children.

Even if we could agree on an exact definition of what men's real interests were and that they have real interests in spending time at home with their children, and even if some men became aware of these real interests, that in itself still might not necessarily increase the freedom of choice for all these men. Keeping in mind the starting point of a patriarchal power structure, then even men who are aware of their 'real interests' might still be afraid to ask their employer's permission for going on parental leave. They know that while employers expect women to eventually go on maternity leave, they do not expect men to take paternity leave. Consequently, requests to go on paternity leave can easily induce a negative reaction from an employer who disapproves of the employee's 'lack of ambition'. Although no scientific studies, to my knowledge, have directly addressed just this problem, studies on workplace culture in Sweden show a correlation between workplace culture and the willingness of men to take paternity leaves (i.e. Haas *et al.* 2002).

Given these structural hindrances, 'daddy months' can actually increase the freedom of choice for many men, as the designation of several months only for the father gives men a stronger bargaining position *vis-à-vis* their employers. Rather than having to defend their 'lack of ambition', fathers can now claim that their family cannot afford to lose several months of leave benefits. Consequently, at least some men find themselves in the ironical position of being forced to do what they really wanted to do anyway, but did not dare to do.

In Sweden some authors try to get around the choice issue altogether by pointing out that all other social insurances in the country are individually based and their benefits cannot be handed over to anyone else, so parental leaves should not be an exception (see the discussions in Lorentzi 2004 and Bergqvist 2008). Each parent should have a set amount of months and they cannot give away these months to anyone else, just as they cannot give away pensions or unemployment insurance to anyone else. Thus, leaves would be shared equally in every family. For example, in Sweden in every family each mother would have six and a half months' leave and each father would have the same leave, and neither parent would be able to decrease the leave time by giving away some time to the other parent.

If we are to take the notion of individuation and postmodern values seriously, however, then it is questionable whether we really want to force the same solution upon every family. No two people have the exact same preferences and needs, so why should everyone be forced to behave in the same way and divide their parental leaves exactly equally? From a feminist perspective, would it really be a problem if, for example, a career-oriented woman had a child with a family-oriented man and they decided that the man should stay at home for most of the leave period so that the mother could pursue her career? If we were to create a non-patriarchal society that no longer forced us into gender roles that prescribe for us how we must behave regardless of our own wants and needs, then why should we assume that everyone would suddenly have the exact same wants and needs? Perhaps, then, the goal of gender equality should not be to make all people exactly equal in their choices, but rather it should be to eliminate the correlation between gender and behaviour.

Even if one accepts this goal, the question is how to get there. Surely, the fastest way to get fathers to share equally in the parental leave time on average is to force them to divide the leave time equally in each case. In the short term parents would lose some freedom of choice, as family-oriented mothers (and perhaps a few family-oriented fathers) would spend less time at home than they would prefer, while some career-oriented fathers (and in some cases also mothers) would spend more time at home than they would prefer. In the long run, however, freedom of choice would increase, as attitudes would start changing and men learn to share in the childrearing and even like it. Once new cultural values become firmly entrenched and employers get used to the fact that on average fathers will go on parental leave for just as long as women, then eventually complete freedom of choice could be reintroduced in the model, as both men and women would be more likely to act in accordance with their 'true' preferences without fear of being punished by their employers, employees or looked down upon by friends, family and neighbours for not being 'good mothers' if they let the fathers stay at home with the children, etc.

For many families, however, the short-term sacrifice in terms of loss of freedom of choice will not be outweighed by the long-term gains to society. We can expect many cases to arise in which families would lose a lot by such a reform, which perhaps is one reason why no government has dared to go so far. Instead, the Icelandic model seems to represent the most politically feasible compromise, where one-third of the leave time is reserved for each parent while the remaining third can be divided according to each family's choice.

Parental Leave Policies and Flexibility

Even if policies that promote gender equality generally seem to increase freedom of choice, such policies can still be formulated in ways that provide more or less freedom of choice by being more or less flexible.

At one extreme, it would be possible to have a parental leave that is open to both parents, but only allows one parent to use it and no possibility exists of staying at home for a longer period and receiving less money per month. At the other extreme, parents could be free to divide their time between themselves as they would like and they can decide to stretch out the leave as long as they like by receiving a lower benefit per month but for more months.

The previous German system approximated to the inflexible model. When the Christian Democratic-liberal coalition government introduced a means-tested, flat-rate childcaring leave after the maternity leave ended, it only allowed mothers to go on this leave. After a man complained to the European Court, the government decided to allow fathers to take this leave as well. However, until 1992 only one parent could take this leave. According to the new law parents could alternate the leave three times, but only one parent could go on leave for a particular period (Rosenkranz et al. 1998: 9). A later law further limited it, so that parents could only divide their stays at home to two periods (Bundesministerium für Familie, Senioren, Frauen und Jugend 2004).

Sweden represents the other extreme, where although some months are reserved for mothers and fathers, parents can choose to divide the remaining months in any way they please, including staying at home during the same period of time but during different days of the week. In addition, parents are free to stretch out the leave as long as they want, so they can, for example, receive half as much payment per month but for twice as many months. In contrast to the previous German system in which parents had to announce how they would divide the parental leave time from the beginning, in the Scandinavian countries parents can also decide at any point in time to change the length of their leave, so a father receiving 25 per cent of the leave money for two months could decide in the third month to receive 100 per cent of it, and then he could decide to return to work in the fifth month and let the mother take care of the child, etc.

Childcare Facilities

Easy and affordable access to high-quality childcare facilities also improves freedom of choice for parents. If they can afford to send their children to day-care centres and if they feel confident that these centres are of high quality, then their chance of returning to work at an earlier stage increases. If access to childcare is combined with generous parental leaves, so that the loss of income from staying at home does not matter much, and the cost of sending children to day care is not high enough to give parents a disincentive to return to work, then parents can make their decisions about how fast to return to work based solely on their own preferences for what is best for their careers, their children and their desire to spend time with their children. Such policies also promote gender equality given the unequal starting point in which the mother is the most likely one to be at home with the children if day care options are not available.

Market liberals might protest that state support for childcare distorts markets and takes away parents' freedom of choice, since the state is likely to favour public day-care centres over private alternatives. Even if this were true, a completely private system strongly restricts freedom of choice for many parents, who cannot afford to pay the high price of day care. For example, a recent survey of childcare in Great Britain complained about 'the shockingly high costs of childcare in Britain' and noted that many parents have trouble paying for it.[4] In America, even the middle class generally finds day care prohibitively expensive. Consequently, rather than send their children to nursery schools with trained personnel, many hire unqualified people, who often are immigrants (including illegal aliens), who do not have any pedagogical training.[5] The question arises as to why one is more 'free' when one feels forced to hire an unqualified, illegal immigrant, but one is less 'free' when one sends one's child to a publicly funded day-care centre, run by university-educated preschool teachers! Even more importantly, why is a mother more free when she feels forced to stay at home although she would like to return to work, but cannot afford day care, but unfree when she is able to decide herself when to return to work, because the childcare facilities are easily affordable?

Nevertheless, market-liberals may have a point that freedom of choice could be improved in countries where public day-care facilities dominate the market. As long as all alternatives remain affordable, it is not clear that they must all be public alternatives. It would be possible to increase freedom of choice by allowing publicly funded private childcare facilities to compete freely with private ones. This would not represent a large deviation from the social democratic model if the private facilities were to be basically publicly financed and had to follow the same rules as public ones concerning fees. Then they would remain affordable and would be forced to compete based on alternative pedagogical philosophies rather than based on being able to provide higher-quality services by charging higher fees.

Alternative Living Styles

So far, I have argued that generous public policies that promote gender equality also promote freedom of choice. Generous parental leave schemes and easy, affordable access to day care obviously also benefit the freedom of choice for single parents (usually mothers) who can both afford to stay at home more easily and are able to return to work more quickly. Such arrangements should also help homosexual couples with children, although certain provisions should be made to allow the non-biological parent to stay at home with a child and receive parental leave benefits if the child is adopted or if the child was born via artificial insemination (in the case of lesbian mothers). When a heterosexual relationship leads to a child and the parents then break up and the mother then enters a lesbian relationship, it still might be good for the child and the father if the father shares in the parental leave time, so in that case it would not matter afterwards whether the mother enters into a homosexual or heterosexual relationship after they break up.

In theory, we would not necessarily expect social democratic countries to be any more tolerant of alternative lifestyles than liberal countries. If we take the free-market economist Milton Friedman's (1980) title to his famous book (co-authored with his wife Rose) at face value, 'free to choose' implies that under a market-liberal regime, the state should stay out of private matters and let people decide themselves how they want to live. Thus, the liberal state should be completely neutral concerning one's choice of lifestyle. In practice, however, countries with social democratic traditions are much more tolerant of alternative lifestyles than countries with liberal traditions, even if liberal countries tend to be more tolerant than conservative ones. Whether the issue is the right to legal abortions (and state-funded ones), the ability to achieve easy, no-fault divorces, the right to same-sex marriage, the right for homosexual couples to adopt children, the ability for couples living together to enjoy the same rights as married couples, etc., the social democratic Scandinavian countries generally have come the farthest in granting freedom of choice. For example, Denmark allows same-sex marriages, while the Swedish government has recently proposed such a law and Sweden also allows homosexual couples to adopt children.

Conclusion

This chapter argues that family policies that promote gender equality as practised in Scandinavia (and especially in Sweden) have also tended to give greater freedom of choice than either liberal or conservative types of policies, by providing greater possibilities to decide how long people want to work or stay at home with their children.

Generous parental leaves make it easier for mothers to decide to stay at home for longer periods than under liberal regimes, while affordable access to day care makes it easier for women to return to work after a shorter period than under conservative regimes. Meanwhile, by providing insurance-based parental leaves that minimize the loss of income when one goes on leave, social democratic types of welfare regimes have also made it easier for fathers to choose to stay at home, since families do not lose much money even if the father earns more money than the mother (which in most families is the case).

Even within the confines of generous parental leave schemes and generous funding of childcare facilities, it is possible to increase the freedom of choice or decrease it. For example, the Swedish parental leave scheme allows for maximum flexibility in that parents can divide the leave time as they like by, for example, deciding to have one parent at home two days a week and the other at home three days a week or by taking a longer leave but receiving a smaller benefit payment per month.

The issue of months reserved for the father brings up an interesting dilemma concerning freedom of choice. In some cases daddy months can actually 'force' the father to do what he would really want to choose, but previously did not dare to choose out of fear of how his employer and work colleagues might react. Furthermore, when fathers are induced to stay at home for longer periods, this can influence the freedom of choice for mothers to return to work earlier and also give children the 'right' to have more time with their fathers, which they presumably would 'choose' to do if they were old enough to make choices.

When it comes to childcare facilities, generous public support increases the freedom of choice of parents by allowing them to decide themselves when they want to return to work. However, the generous public support does not necessarily have to go solely to public childcare facilities. Public support can just as well go to private or cooperative facilities as long as these alternative facilities are forced to have the same pricing model as the public facilities to insure that good-quality care remains available to all regardless of income. Instead, policies should be geared to allowing competition among competing pedagogical concepts of what kinds of activities the children should engage in, which gives parents greater freedom of choice in deciding what kind of day care they would choose for their children.

Finally, if we take the concept of freedom of choice seriously, then we should also have maximum freedom to choose our lifestyles. This includes whether to live together or get married; whether to have homosexual or heterosexual relationships (and marriages); whether to live with a partner or alone; whether to raise our children with the other parent or alone; whether to stay married or get divorced; whether to have a child or choose to have an abortion, etc. Even though, in principle, countries with liberal traditions should support maximum choice in these areas, in practice social democratic Scandinavian countries have been much more tolerant than the liberal, Anglo-Saxon countries.

Acknowledgements

The research for this chapter was financed by grants from the Baltic Sea Foundation in Sweden for the project 'Family Policies in Post-communist Europe: Influence from the Swedish or German Model?' and from the Czech Grant Agency for the project 'The Revenge of History? An Examination of the Historical Roots of Childcare, Healthcare and Elderly Care Policies in the Czech Republic', grant number GA403/09/1182; and Grant no. IAA700280901 from the Czech Academy of Science Grant Agency.

Notes

1. Unfortunately, this question was asked in the 1994 survey but not repeated in the 2002 survey. Nevertheless, no reason exists to assume that the results would change much if the question had been asked in the 2002 survey, since, for example, the percentage of women thinking that women should contribute to the family income increased for most European countries (i.e. Saxonberg and Sirovátka 2006).
2. Heitlinger (1993) calls this 'maternal feminism'.
3. For the recent German reforms, see Bundesregierung (2007).
4. The quote comes from Daycare Trust (2008: 4), but the problem of affordability is discussed throughout the report.
5. See, for example, Esping-Andersen (1999: 57, fn. 7), who admits that Americans usually use 'cheap informal care from unlicensed women', but he makes no mention of the usage of immigrants and illegal aliens.

References

Batljan, I., Tillander, S., Ljungh, S. Ö. and Sjöström, M. (2004), Föräldrapenning, pappornas uttag av dagar, fakta och analys [Parental leave allowances, the utilization of leave days by fathers, facts and analyisis], Swedish Government Ministry of Social Affairs, p. 7. Available at: www.regeringen.se/content/1/c6/01/77/14/116bbfe1.pdf.

Beck, U. and Beck-Gernsheim, E. (2001), *Individualization: Institutionalized Individualism and its Social and Political Consequences*, London: Sage.

Beck, U. and Beck-Gernsheim, E. (1992), *Risk Society: Towards a New Modernity*, London: Sage.

Bergqvist, C. (2008), The political debate about gender equality and earmarking the parental leave for fathers in the Nordic countries. Paper presented at the Annual RC19 Conference, 4–6 September.

Bundesministerium für Familie, Senioren, Frauen und Jugend (2004), Bericht über die Auswirkungen der §§ 15 und 16 Bundeserziehungsgeldgesetz [Report on the influence of law paragraphs 15 and 16 of the Law on Federal Childcaring Allowances]. Available at: www.treffpunkteltern.de/article.php?sid=306 (accessed 25 January 2009).

Bundesregierung (2007), Reformprojekte Elterngeld [Reform project parental leave allowances]. Available at: www.bundesregierung.de/nn_66124/Content/DE/StatischeSeiten/Breg/Reformprojekte/familienpolitik-2006-08-21-elterngeld1.html (accessed 9 December 2007).

Daycare Trust (2008), *Childcare Cost Survey 2008*, London: Daycare Trust.

Deutsches Jugendinstitut (2008), Kindertagesbetreuung im Spiegel der Statistik: Zahlenspiegel 2007 [Childcare reflected in statistics]. Available at: www.bmfsfj.de/

bmfsfj/generator/RedaktionBMFSFJ/Abteilung5/Pdf-Anlagen/Zahlenspiegel200
7,property=pdf,bereich=,sprache=de,rwb=true.pd.

Esping-Andersen, G. (1999), *Social Foundations of Postindustrial Economies*, Oxford: Oxford University Press.

Friedman, M. and Friedman, R. (1980), *Free to Choose*, London: Secker and Warburg.

Giddens, A. (1991), *Modernity and Self-identity*, Cambridge: Polity Press.

Haas, L., Allard, K. and Hwang, P. (2002), The impact of organizational culture on men's use of parental leave in Sweden, *Community, Work and Family*, 5, 3: 319–42.

Hakim, C. (2000), *Work–Lifestyle Choices in the 21st Century: Preference Theory*, Oxford: Oxford University Press.

Heitlinger, A. (1993), The impact of the transition from communism on the status of women in the Czech and Slovak republics. In N. Funk and M. Mueller (eds), *Gender Politics and Post-Communism: Reflections from Eastern Europe and the Former Soviet Union*, New York and London: Routledge, pp. 95–109.

Lewis, J. (ed.) (1993), *Women and Social Policies in Europe*, Cheltenham: Edward Elgar.

Lorentzi, U. (2004), *Vems Valfrihet – Debattbok för en delad föräldraförsäkring* [Whose freedom of choice – Debate book for a shared parental leave insurance], Stockholm: Agora.

Lukes, S. (1974/87) *Power: A Radical View*, London: Macmillan Education.

OECD (2007), OECD Family Database. Available at: www.oecd.org/els/social/family/database (accessed 22 November 2007).

Rosenkranz, D., Rost, H. and Schröter, A. (1998), *Väter und Erziehungsurlaub* [Fathers and child-raising leave], IFB Materialien Nr. 7–96, Staatsinstitut für Familienforschung an der Universität Bamberg, Germany.

Sainsbury, D. (ed.) (1994), *Gendering Welfare States*, London: Sage.

Sainsbury, D. (1999), Social democratic welfare states. In D. Sainsbury (ed.), *Gender and the Welfare States Regimes*, Oxford: Oxford University Press, pp. 75–116.

Saxonberg, S. and Sirovátka, T. (2006), Failing family policy in post-communist central Europe, *Journal of Comparative Policy Analysis*, 8, 2: 185–202.

SCB (2008), Uttag av föräldrapenning och tillfällig föräldrapenning 1974–2007 [Utilization of parental leave allowances and temporary parental leave allowances]. Available at: www.scb.se/templates/tableOrChart____27563.asp (accessed 23 January 2009).

Index

Abel-Smith, Brian   19
activation policies   67, 94, 100
adverse selection   23, 110, 123
  health insurance   114–16
  impact of exit options on   109
  most effective means of dealing with   14
  pensions   119
  possible consequences in relation to   3
  solidarity and   111–12
  unemployment insurance   120–1
agency problems   29
Akerlof, G. A.   12
ambulant care   78, 79, 80, 81, 82, 85, 86, 88
  entitlement to   84
  family care supplemented by   87
Anglo-Saxon model   63, 64, 109, 136
APA (*Allocation Personnalisée à*
  l'Autonomie)   98–9
Appleby, J.   5, 10, 14
appointment times   28–9
Arkansas   99
artificial insemination   135
asymmetric knowledge   29
Austria   97, 99, 100, 101, 105
authoritarianism   131

Bailey, S. J.   14, 15
Baker, T.   111
Baldock, J.   9
Ball, S.   37
Bartlett, W.   13, 19, 20, 21, 22
Batljan, I.   131
Becker, Gary   81
benefits   47, 56, 62, 82
  comprehensive   112
  declining   52
  differentiated   51
  in kind   79
  means-tested   98, 129, 133
  retirement   117
  unemployment   53, 54, 65, 68, 111, 120
Bergqvist, C.   132
Berlusconi, Silvio   63
Bettio, F.   97, 99

black markets   98, 104
Blair, Tony   6
Blank, Florian   2
Bleses, P.   47
Blomqvist, P.   5, 48, 63, 64, 114
Bluem, Norbert   80
blue-collar workers   50, 52
Böckmann, R.   51
Bode, I.   6, 7, 77, 79
bounded rationality   21
Bruttel, O.   48
Burgess, S.   36
Butler, T.   37

care   9, 10, 20, 77–93
  cash for   3, 94–108
  disorganization of   6
  feminized   96, 102
  good-quality   9
  irrationality in   21
  long-term   1, 46, 47, 48, 49, 53, 54, 58,
    77
  see also ambulant care; childcare; family
    care; health-care policy; long-term care
    insurance; social care
Career Guard (Canadian insurance
  firm)   121
Cash and Counseling Demonstration
  pilots   99
CDU (German Christian Democratic
  Party)   80, 130, 133
centre-left/centre-right governments   64,
  66, 67, 74
childcare   82, 97, 100, 128, 133–5, 136
Chiu, W. H.   121
choice-and-competition model   25, 29, 31
'choose and book' system   28
citizen-consumers   46, 56
citizenship   100
  opening up opportunities   104
  social   62–76, 96, 106
  well-being and   103–4, 105
Clarke, J.   7, 46, 48, 77
Clasen, J.   120, 121

Jordan, B. 6, 7, 12, 13
junk meals 7

Kaps, P. 52–3
Karni, E. 121
Kemmerling, A. 48
Kemp, P. A. 103
Kim, W. 121
kindergartens 129
Klünder, M. 82
Knaus, T. 116
Knight, Jim 41
Knijn, T. 86
Köppe, S. 59
Kremer, M. 48
Kuhlmann, E. 48, 50

Labour government (UK) 20, 26, 30
labour markets 77, 106, 118, 129
  black/grey 98, 99, 102, 105
  flexibilization of 67
  freeing up 'unpaid' carers to participate
    in 100
laws/legislative decrees (Italy) 66, 69, 71
league tables (school performance) 36, 37,
    39, 41, 42
learning-disabled adults 102, 103
Lega Nord (Italy) 63, 64
Le Grand, Julian 2, 5, 6, 10, 12, 13, 15,
    19–32, 36, 37, 41, 43
Leiber, M. 48, 51
Leibfried, S. 47
lesbian mothers 135
Lewis, J. 78, 96, 99, 125
liberalism 131
life expectancy 119
lifestyles 125, 136
  alternative 135
  freedom to choose 4
  healthier 31
Lipsey, David 19, 29, 31
living standards 8
local authorities 78, 81
Lombardy model 68, 71, 72
London 26–7
London Patient Choice 30
long-term care insurance 51–2, 55, 81
  effects of 83
Long-Term Care Insurance Act
    (Germany 1995/1996) 78–80, 84, 86,
    87–8
Lorentzi, U. 132
loyalty 2, 23, 35
Lucey, H. 37
Lukes, S. 131

Maastricht Treaty (1992) 63, 69
Mager, H.-C. 84

male-breadwinner model 78, 82, 99, 128,
    130
Mann, K. 5, 14
Manouguian, M.-S. 48, 51
Marical, F. 14
market-based reform 2, 31
market-enhancing reforms 46, 48, 58
market inefficiencies 25
marketization 4, 5, 9, 46, 47, 58, 59, 88, 96,
    106
markets 3, 7, 30, 36, 47–9
  access to 55
  allowing institutions to fail 28
  claimed abolition of 26
  created outside existing systems 58
  difference between 53
  incentives for players too weak 26
  limited because of uncertainty of
    demand 23
  moving delivery from state to 9
  new dividing lines caused by the use of
    4
  officially obligating citizens to participate
    in 54
  private sector incentivized to enter 27
  provision might lead to
    underprovision 24
  role of 54
  social policy and 31
  state support for childcare distorts
    134
  time taken to develop 9
  unregulated 23, 98
  see also competitive market forces;
    quasi-markets
Martin, C. 47
Martin, J. 36
Marxists 131
maternity leave 127–30
MAXQDA (text analysis tool) 85
Mayring, P. 85
Medicaid 99
Milburn, Alan 30
Ministero del Welfare (Italy) 66, 67
Ministry of Work and Social Affairs
    (Germany) 52
modernization 67, 68, 69, 73, 74
monopoly 9, 23
  public 25, 52, 58
  purchasing power 24
monopsony 24
moral hazard 23, 121
moral responsibility 83–4, 88
Morris, J. 95, 96, 100
Mossialos, E. 6, 14, 65, 111, 112
motivation 12, 13, 20, 22
multidimensional quality 35, 37, 39, 40, 41,
    42, 43